CIVIL WAR VIRGINIA
Battleground for a Nation

Civil War Virginia
Battleground
for a Nation

James I. Robertson, Jr.

University Press of Virginia

Charlottesville and London

THE UNIVERSITY PRESS OF VIRGINIA
Copyright © 1991 by the Rector and Visitors
of the University of Virginia

First published 1991

Library of Congress Cataloging-in-Publication Data
Robertson, James I.
Civil War Virginia: battleground for a nation / James I. Robertson, Jr.
   p.   cm.
Includes bibliographical references.
ISBN 0-8139-1296-2
  1. Virginia—History—Civil War, 1861–1865. I. Title.
E534.9.R62   1990
973.7'09755—dc20   90-38536
                                                              CIP

Printed in the United States of America

Contents

Preface

No other state has ever undergone the trauma through which Virginia passed in the Civil War. As the Mother State of the nation, Virginia played a leading role in the birth and early years of the Republic. Then, in 1861, the Old Dominion found itself literally in the middle of approaching hostilities between North and South. Virginia had powerful Southern sympathies but also a strong attachment to the Union.

An independent Confederate States of America took shape. Historian Bruce Catton has stated: "The new Southern nation that was struggling to be born needed Virginia as a man needs the breath of life." Without Virginia, the Confederacy could not hope to win a war. With Virginia, the young nation had a chance.

The state was among the last to join the Southern experiment in independence. Virginia had to endure being the major battleground of the bloodiest war in American history; its capital became the primary target of Union might. Cities were ravaged, lands laid waste, factories and homes destroyed, tens of thousands of its citizens killed, a third of its territory was lost.

Today three dozen surviving battlefields are mute testimony to the struggle for Virginia. More than 265 monuments in the state are silent reminders of the gallantry and sacrifice necessary to weld the nation together. In 1958 Virginia's General Assembly proclaimed that "it shall be the policy of the State to perpetuate a knowledge of the deeds and traditions of a valiant people, who through the terrible ordeal of a great war, forged one nation, undivided, under God."

This is the story of that terrible ordeal. This booklet seeks to fill a long-standing need for a capsule-history of Virginia's pivotal and heroic role in the Civil War. It is intended both as a supplement to *Civil War Sites in Virginia: A Tour Guide*, published by the University Press of Virginia, and as a replacement for the smaller, long out-of-print *Virginia, 1861–1865: Iron Gate to the Confederacy*, a military summary that I wrote in 1961 for the Virginia Civil War Commission. I am most grateful to the Virginia State Library and Archives for permission to quote extensively from that work.

Any historical study is the product of more than one individual's efforts. Such was the case here. My deep thanks go to longtime friends and colleagues who volunteered to read the original draft. Charles P. Roland of the University of Kentucky and Gary W. Gallagher of Pennsylvania State University went through the entire manuscript with a critical eye. Ludwell H. Johnson of the College of William and Mary and Sandra V. Parker of Richmond likewise read selected portions. Each made valuable suggestions for improvement. However, I alone am responsible for any factual errors.

Guy R. Swanson and Corrine Hudgins of the Museum of the Confederacy were, as always, gracious and helpful in supplying some of the illustrations. Personnel in the Virginia Tech Media Productions Services—Photographs worked diligently to provide sharp reproductions of other pictures used. A stipend from the College of Arts and Sciences, plus a grant from the Frank L. Curtis Fund at Virginia Tech, defrayed most of the research costs.

John McGuigan, Acquisitions Editor of the University Press of Virginia, was a source of encouragement and assistance throughout this project. My wife Libba, chief assistant and best friend, oversaw the conversion of scribbled pages into readable computer printouts—all the while wondering aloud if I would ever master modern gadgetry.

This book is dedicated to the more than 125 people from all across the nation who annually attend Virginia Tech's "Campaigning with Lee" summer seminar. No group of Civil War enthusiasts could possess more comradery, devotion, and generosity. They call themselves "Bud's Brigade"; I call them treasured friends.

Harpers Ferry, at the confluence of the Potomac and Shenandoah rivers, and its federal arsenal. *Harper's Weekly*

. I .

War Clouds Gather

On Sunday evening, October 16, 1859, as darkness settled over the quiet Virginia mountains, a band of sixteen whites and five blacks left the Maryland farmhouse where they had been hiding for several weeks. The heavily armed men headed southward down a deserted country road. Their leader was the fiery if not unbalanced abolitionist John Brown; their mission was to seize the store of arms in the federal arsenal across the Potomac River at Harpers Ferry, Virginia; their goal was to incite all slaves in the area to rebel against their masters and join Brown's group. Then, like Joshua leading the Israelites in the conquest of Canaan, Brown planned to drive through Virginia, Tennessee, and Alabama. The campaign would trigger a chain reaction of slave uprisings throughout the Deep South and by bloodshed end the curse of bondage.

For forty years Northerners and Southerners had first debated with and then derided each other over the issue of slavery. The time for talking had passed, Brown concluded. The time for action was at hand.

Brown's raid lasted thirty-six hours. It was amateurish in design and a failure in execution. Federal troops quickly arrived and stormed the small enginehouse where the band had taken refuge. Several of the raiders were killed. Brown and six survivors were arrested, convicted of insurrection and murder, then hanged.

Passions over Brown's act ran high in Virginia. To

John Brown (1800–1859). Alfred H.
Guernsey, *Harper's Pictorial History
of the Great Rebellion* (New York,
1866–68)

many residents of the South, this was the last straw.
Physical invasion of a state had occurred. Four innocent
citizens had been slain, including a free black. An overt
move had been made to promote revolution within the
Old Dominion.

Equally as ominous, many Northerners from the beginning openly praised John Brown's crime as something Virginia deserved. Abolitionist orator Wendell
Phillips thundered to an audience that Virginia was a
land without a government. "She is only a chronic insurrection!" he shouted. "She is a pirate ship, and John
Brown sails the sea a Lord High Admiral of the Al-

mighty with his commission to sink every pirate he meets on God's ocean!"

Such voices from the North caused the Richmond *Whig* to fire a late October volley of its own: "There are thousands of men in our midst who, a month ago, scoffed at the idea of a dissolution of the Union as a madman's dream, but who now hold the opinion that [the nation's] days are numbered, its glory perished."

That was no empty statement. As John Brown's ghost stalked the South in the months thereafter, states reorganized and strengthened their militia. Dozens of Virginia communities began forming home-guard units against attacks from other John Browns. At a mass meeting in southside Virginia, for example, forty-seven volunteers sprang forward to form a company "to protect the homes, the families and firesides, the honor and interest of the citizens of Danville and its vicinity, from invasion from without and insurrection from within." Meanwhile, increasing numbers of Southerners in other states wondered aloud how much longer they could tolerate union with a North which continually flaunted the law.

In January 1860 John Letcher of Lexington succeeded the tobacco-chewing firebrand Henry A. Wise as governor. Letcher, a thorough law-and-order executive, earnestly wanted Virginia to stay in the Union if it could do so with honor. The Old Dominion watched, listened, and hoped throughout that year. In November the long-dreaded chain reaction began when Abraham Lincoln won election as president of the United States.

Lincoln's victory came almost exclusively with Northern votes. Fear and anger swept through the South following the presidential election. Lincoln's Republican party, spawned amid the slavery controversies of the mid–1850s, appeared in the South as a seedbed for abolitionism by force. Republican opposition to any extension of slavery beyond its present boundaries seemed to be an attempt to isolate the South from the rest of the nation. Hence, Southerners interpreted the 1860 election as the first step by Republicans toward the ultimate economic and political subjugation of the South.

Emotion now took the place of reason. On December 20, amid an atmosphere of fireworks, parades, and rallies, South Carolina seceded from the Union. Six other Southern states followed suit in as many weeks. Oratorical lightning bolts flashed across the darkening skies of the Deep South as the "United States of America," in business since 1789, ceased to exist.

The first maddening weeks of 1861 saw Virginia make every effort to restore the Union. The state's geographical position squarely between North and South made it a buffer as well as a potential battleground. Social and economic links with both sections placed Virginia even more in the middle of the dispute. Moderation and tradition seemed the only routes to avert disaster. On January 7 Governor Letcher summoned the state legislature into extra session. "Surely," he told the delegates, "no people have been more blessed than we have been, and it is melancholy to think that all is now about to be sacrificed on the Altar of Passion."

Letcher secured legislative approval for two actions. First, he followed the lead of other Southern states by calling for the election of a secession convention to monitor the course of events and to make recommendations on Virginia's status within the Union.

The governor's second move was to call for a national peace convention that would discuss all alternatives to schism and war. On February 4, 1861—the same day

Governor John Letcher (1813–
1884). Eleanor S. Brockenbrough
Library, The Museum of the
Confederacy, Richmond

that delegates from the seceded states met to organize a
Southern nation and Virginia voters went to the polls to
pick representatives for the secession convention—the
Peace Conference held its first session in Washington,
D.C. Chairing the assembly was an aged Virginian, former president John Tyler, who had held every elective
federal office during his long public career. A total of
132 delegates from twenty-one states were in attendance.

   This last-minute effort to avoid national conflict was
doomed from the start because compromise no longer
functioned as a national adhesive. Republican leaders
insisted that the spread of slavery across the land must
cease; Southerners demanded that the legal protections

of slavery be recognized and the system be allowed to extend to new areas where it might flourish. Neither side would budge. The Peace Conference produced a series of shaky resolutions and then adjourned in failure.

Abraham Lincoln watched Virginia closely as winter turned to spring. So did Jefferson Davis, the former senator from Mississippi who in February had been unanimously elected president of the Confederate States of America. Virginia's citizens remained divided in sentiment. Some were ready to leave the Union at once; others wanted reconciliation on any honorable terms. Many Virginians felt resentment against South Carolina for precipitating the crisis. A sizable number of the state's citizens were angry at the Lincoln administration for heating up an already-hot situation with a combination of foot-dragging and veiled threats.

The Richmond *Whig* on March 6, 1861, voiced the opinion that the Deep South states had acted rashly; "but, considering them erring sisters entitled to our sympathies, and our aid in an emergency, Virginia can never consent, and will never consent for the Federal Government to employ coercive measures toward them." John Esten Cooke, a Virginia writer who was to become the most famous Confederate novelist, stated that same day: "We'll fight our way out yet, and crush the miserable intrigants who are stifling the brave old commonwealth—for brave I do believe she is at heart. God defend the right!"

The Virginia Convention, elected in early February, consisted of 152 members. A majority of them were unionists, but "unionists" in Virginia had a meaning of its own. Those delegates were not opposed to secession in principle; they were against their state using this instrument which they regarded as a last, extreme measure.

On the other hand, the Virginia legislature, convention, and governor were of like mind on one crucial issue: the federal government had no right to employ force against a state which wished to leave the Union. Governor Letcher stated publicly as early as January 1861 that any attempt by Federal troops to pass through Virginia for the purpose of coercing any Southern state would be treated by Virginia as an act of invasion. Since Union soldiers could not easily march into the South without somewhere crossing the Old Dominion's borders, Letcher's pronouncement was something not to be taken lightly.

Although the Virginia Convention rejected secession by a two-to-one margin on April 4, tensions increased and war enthusiasm continued to mount. A showdown neared at Charleston, S.C., between Confederate forces and the besieged Federal garrison inside Fort Sumter. On April 12, with a Northern relief expedition approaching the harbor, Southern batteries opened fire. Fort Sumter surrendered after a thirty-six-hour bombardment.

Virginia's balmy spring turned to summer's heat when news arrived of the activities at Charleston. People in Richmond took to the streets in celebration. Word of Sumter's fall "was like a volcano bursting forth in the center" of the capital, a schoolteacher commented. Voices and bands vied for attention. The Fayette Artillery fired a 100-gun salute from Capitol Square "in honor of the victory." A large throng lowered the American flag from the roof of the Capitol and replaced it with a Confederate ensign. Rockets filled the night air.

Tar barrels burned as torch-carrying crowds staged nighttime secession marches. Many such parades purposefully swung by St. John's Church, where seventy-five years earlier Patrick Henry had thundered: "Give me liberty or give me death!"

On April 15 Lincoln called on the states for 75,000 militia to put down an insurrection "too powerful to be suppressed by the ordinary course of judicial proceedings." Virginia's quota was 8,000 men. Yet by then disunion sentiment in the state "was at white heat," one visitor declared. Lincoln's request for troops was a Northern acceptance of a challenge to civil war. That call was also the breaking point for the Old Dominion. "Lincoln declares war on the South," the Richmond *Examiner* warned, "and his Secretary demands from Virginia a quota of cutthroats to desolate Southern firesides." The Richmond *Whig* concluded: "Lincoln gives us no alternative but to fight or run."

Northern coercion and Southern traditions now made secession palatable in Virginia. Governor Letcher refused to honor Lincoln's troop request. The secession convention spent two days in intense debate. Longwinded speeches about state rights and slaveholders' liberties influenced some delegates; yet swaying the majority was the threat of invasion of the state by Federal forces.

Feelings were mixed and emotional at the April 17 vote. One delegate opposed to secession "broke down in incoherent sobs"; another favoring withdrawal from the Union "wept like a child." Then came the roll call. The vote was 88–55 in favor of secession. Delegates set May 18 as the date for voters to approve the ordinance, solemnly shook hands with one another, and headed home.

By declaration Virginia was now a free and independent state. Like its Southern sisters, it felt that secession was a peaceful act. Federal laws no longer applied inside its borders. Virginians were defending their inherent rights and liberties. They would fight only if attacked.

Commensurate with the ordinance of secession, Letcher received authorization to call into military service as many volunteers as needed to "repel invasion and protect the citizens of the state in the present emergency." Letcher kept this mobilization measure secret for three days because he had already dispatched troops to seize two installations vital to the safety and freedom of Virginia.

On April 18, 1,000 state militia converged on the large federal arsenal at Harpers Ferry. It contained the only rifle-making machinery south of the Potomac River. Only forty-seven Regular Army soldiers defended the works. They hastily set fire to the buildings and fled. The Virginians just as quickly extinguished the flames. Because it was closely surrounded on all sides by mountains, Harpers Ferry was indefensible. Some $2 million worth of machinery was therefore transferred to Richmond, along with several thousand new rifles.

At the same time, an even larger contingent of Virginia militia surrounded Gosport Navy Yard at Norfolk. It was the nation's leading naval base, as well as the largest shipbuilding and repair facility in the South. Some 10 vessels and 1,200 cannon were stored there. The small garrison was under the command of an aged officer bewildered by what was happening and ignored by authorities in Washington.

On the night of April 20, he ordered the yard put to the torch and the vessels scuttled. The operation was bungled. Virginia troops occupied the yard, seized most

Gosport Navy Yard afire in mid-April 1861. Paul F. Mottelay, *The Soldier in Our Civil War* (New York, 1884–85)

of the artillery, and acquired more gunpowder (2,800 barrels) than the Confederate States of America possessed at the moment. One of the partially scuttled ships, the USS *Merrimack*, was subsequently rebuilt and became the Confederacy's most famous war vessel.

Virginia could not survive as an independent country. Letcher and his administration planned to link the state to the Confederacy when the people on May 18 ratified secession. Yet to wait until then for a political certainty

(Virginians approved the ordinance by a four-to-one margin) created the danger of the state being overrun and occupied by Federal forces. Therefore, Virginia and Confederate officials moved to form an alliance.

Confederate vice president Alexander H. Stephens rushed to Richmond. On April 24 Virginia officially became part of the Confederate States of America. Three days later, partly out of Confederate gratitude and partly because of its unrivaled value as a manufacturing center, Richmond became the capital of the new nation.

Forty years of controversy over slavery spawned the Civil War. Virginia was one of the staunchest defenders of the system. The first blacks in the English colonies had arrived in 1619 at Jamestown. Slavery became an economic way of life to generations of Virginia's early settlers.

Following the 1831 Nat Turner uprising in Southampton County—a murderous spree by slaves which left fifty-five whites dead and twenty-one blacks subsequently executed—new "black laws" tightly restricted the movements of all blacks and further strengthened the institution of slavery. By 1860 Virginia contained more slaves (490,000) than any other Southern state. Yet the system was not evenly distributed in the Old Dominion.

No more than a fourth of all white Virginians on the eve of civil war had a direct involvement with slavery. The institution was heavily concentrated in the tidewater and the southside, where the majority of the white population, the root of political power, was likewise based. Slavery unquestionably was the major issue in the breakup of the Union, but other factors of near-equal importance influenced Virginia's course in the secession crisis.

The United States at that time existed more in name than in fact. It was not that Virginians loved the nation less, but that they loved their native state more. The host of military officers who offered their swords to the Confederacy did so because their beloved Virginia had become a Confederate state.

Decades of abolitionist attacks on the South in general, years of tariff and economic pressures from Northern business interests, repeated verbal assaults on state sovereignty in the face of Virginia's deep-rooted belief in self-government, an 1859 invasion of the state by an abolitionist terrorist who went to his death hailed in the North as a saint, Lincoln's mobilization of troops to force seceded Southern states back into an undesired Union—all of these issues led Virginia to abandon the nation it had done so much to create.

Virginia was the first of the English colonies and therefore the "Mother of States." After achieving independence, the new states had formed a nation whose framework took a long time to form and whose national mold required a century to harden. No state during that period exceeded Virginia in nurturing the fledgling country. Patrick Henry ("The Trumpet of Liberty"), George Washington ("The Father of His Country"), Thomas Jefferson ("Author of the Declaration of Independence"), James Madison ("The Father of the Constitution"), and John Marshall ("The Greatest Chief Justice") had led an array of Virginians who made the United States a reality. For more than half the years of the Republic before the Civil War, someone from the Old Dominion had occupied the presidency. In 1860 one of every sixteen native Americans claimed Virginia as the family birthplace.

The state possessed many ties with the North. Sons of

Virginia frequently went north to study at Yale, Harvard, Columbia, Princeton, and West Point. Virginia families often journeyed north to vacation in summertime. North-South marriages in Virginia were commonplace. Nevertheless, the state was Southern in tradition and sentiments.

In April 1861 two sections went to war fighting for the same thing: America, as each side envisioned what the nation ought to be. Four days after Virginia seceded, a local militia company in Richmond, the Governor's Guard, decided to spend the night on the Capitol grounds. It had rained that day; the ground was damp and chilly. Private Henry Tucker caught a cold which rapidly triggered pneumonia and death. Tucker was the first soldier to die on Virginia soil as a result of the war. His passing hardly seemed like a heroic beginning for America's greatest struggle.

. II .

Caught in the Middle

In large measure the Southern Confederacy lasted as long as it did because of the resources and steadfastness of Virginia. For four years the state was the principal target of Union military might; for four years its lands and communities, fathers and sons, as well as its women and children, felt the brutal hand of war as no other section of this nation has ever known it. Virginia stood firm and defiant in the Civil War until little else remained. The Confederacy experienced defeat after Virginia experienced destruction.

Simple geography, the state's wealth, and its traditional ties to the South doomed Virginia to the fate it suffered. The Old Dominion was the most exposed of the Confederate States. It was the size of New England, with some of its counties in 1861 extending to the Ohio River. The very shape of the state was like a spear thrusting itself into the heart of the North. Only the Potomac River separated Virginia from the capital of the North.

At the outbreak of the Civil War, Virginia was in the main a rural state of tobacco, livestock, orchards, and grain. The cities were mostly large towns, with open country beginning at the end of the streets. The scores of dirt roads crisscrossing the state were bottomless pits in wet weather. Roads planked by wooden boards were hazardous in any climate. Yet the major roads would become inviting avenues of invasion for Federal columns, while lesser-used highways would serve as the floor-lines for earthworks.

In addition, by 1861 Virginia had achieved a level of prestige which made it critically important to both North and South. It was the largest, richest, and most populous of the Southern states. Virginia had more white inhabitants (1,105,000) and more military-age whites (196,500) than any of its southern sisters. The state's industrial capacity was nearly as great as that of the seven original Confederate States combined. Virginia produced almost a third of the South's manufactured goods. Its iron production was three times that of the next Southern state. Fully 20 percent of the South's railroad mileage lay within the Old Dominion.

Other assets made Virginia pivotal in the war. Most of the South's iron, coal, salt, and lead were mined there. Virginia had a principal seaport (Norfolk) and the largest navy yard in the South. Virginia also had Richmond, the state capital and the closest thing to a manufacturing center in the lower half of the nation.

Richmond was a sprawling and beautiful city. Built on seven hills overlooking the falls of the James River and situated between the plantations of the tidewater and the farms of the piedmont, it contained 38,000 residents. Richmond was the South's third largest city and the largest in manufacturing output.

While fifty-two tobacco companies had formed Richmond's economic base for years, iron manufacture by 1860 had become the city's principal asset. Inside that one urban area were fourteen foundries, six rolling mills, six iron railing plants, and fifty iron-and-metal works. The largest of these plants was the Tredegar Iron Works snuggled beside the Kanawha Canal. It became more than "the mother arsenal of the Confederacy";

Tredegar was the industrial heart of the South, attested by the almost 1,100 cannon that it produced during the war. The Richmond Armory could turn out 5,000 small arms per month. Nearby was an armament plant—later known as the Confederate States Laboratory—which could manufacture everything from an occasional artillery piece to percussion caps.

Richmond had eight flour mills, of which Gallego was

Richmond in 1861. *Harper's Pictorial History of the Great Rebellion*

the world's largest. The city was also one of America's leading transportation centers. In addition to being an international port, the state capital was the terminus for the 200-mile canal connecting it with the western part of Virginia. Its five railroads spread in every direction. If Richmond and the surrounding Henrico County had been a state, that one Virginia precinct would have ranked sixth among Southern states in industrial production.

Richmond became the arsenal of the Confederacy.

This in turn made it the chief target of Federal military operations. On a map it looked simple: Richmond was only 110 miles from Washington and the might of the North. Yet there was a good deal more to the story. An enemy would need a week to make the overland march unimpeded. However, if Confederate gunboats and shore batteries could hold back Union naval threats up the rivers, and with the Allegheny Mountains a natural western barrier, Federal forces would have to advance southward along a 100-mile corridor full of advantages for the defenders. Numerous rivers and creeks ran in a west-east direction; swampy areas near the coast hampered mass movements; the rolling piedmont country of central Virginia contained dense forests, wide stretches of open country, and slightly elevated ground here and there, offered ideal fields of fire. Hence, the Northern battle cry "On to Richmond!" became a siren's song, enticing one Federal army after another to march southward onto a giant killing-ground.

All of that would come in time. The latter half of April 1861 saw Virginia—and the rest of the nation— in a flurry of activity as the two sides mobilized for what almost everyone thought would be a short war. Life assumed an unknown excitement. Everything was new and unsettled and tentative. Choosing sides was the first order of business for many Virginians.

Of the state's officers of field and general grade in the Regular Army, as many remained with the Union as joined the Confederacy. A total of 104 Virginians rose to the rank of general in the Southern armies. Among the number who rushed to Richmond in those first days of civil war were some of that conflict's most noted personalities.

One was a profoundly devout and eccentric Virginia

An artist's drawing of Manassas Junction, with troops and earthworks protecting the railroad. *The Soldier in Our Civil War*

The Tredegar Iron Works in Richmond, shown in an 1865 photograph published for the first time. Library of Congress

Military Institute professor known to the cadets as "Tom Fool" Jackson. He was a humorless man, slovenly of dress, and one who had heretofore given few hints of the military genius that he was shortly to unveil. He would lead a group of VMI cadets to Richmond, where they were to drill militia recruits; and from that day until he was mortally wounded, the man they would call "Stonewall" never took a furlough or spent a night away from his troops.

Another officer was a twenty-nine-year-old, fun-loving lieutenant who was redheaded and powerfully built. An enormous beard and ornate uniforms reflected a dramatic flair. Boundless energy seemed one of his leading characteristics. He abstained from alcohol and profanity, and in time he became a magnificent leader of mounted troops. Some friends called him "Beauty," but most acquaintances knew him by the initials of his given names, "Jeb" Stuart.

Joseph E. Johnston, quartermaster general of the U.S. Army in 1860, was a thoroughly trained professional soldier. Soundly analytical most times, he was defense-minded at all times. This "fiery, gray-goateed bantam" was highbred and peppery. He got along well with his subordinates, not so well with his equals, and not well at all with his superior, President Jefferson Davis.

Young George E. Pickett, a confirmed romantic with hair curled and perfumed, had high military ambitions. Graduating at the bottom of his West Point class was not an asset.

John B. Magruder was an older officer. His appearance and flair for the dramatic had earned him the nickname "Prince John," but his military credentials seemed solid.

A. Powell Hill, thinner than most men, had cold eyes

and chestnut hair worn long. He possessed an illness which became progressively worse through the war years. Yet from the beginning Hill reflected the dash and spirit of the fighter that he was.

Mild-mannered but internationally known, Matthew Fontaine Maury had pioneered the study of oceanography in his Washington observatory. He too brought his talents to Virginia.

And then there was Lee.

In 1861 Robert E. Lee was a professional soldier with more than thirty years of distinguished service behind him. Many thought the fifty-four-year-old colonel to be the nation's finest soldier. He was strongly built, with a manly bearing which made him seem taller than 5 feet, 10 inches. A dark mustache and graying hair added to his impressive appearance. With superb patience and an extraordinary knowledge of military matters, Lee possessed all of the characteristics of the consummate soldier.

Viscount Wolseley, commander in chief of the British army, was with Lee several times during the war. Wolseley later stated: "I have met many of the great men of my time, but Lee alone impressed me with the feeling that I was in the presence of a man who was cast in a grander mould, and made of different and of finer metal than all other men."

Which way Lee would go in this civil war was a personal matter critical to both North and South. On April 18 Lee declined an informal offer to command all Union forces. He resigned from the U.S. Army at the same time. As Lee stated earlier to a Northern friend, "I cannot raise my hand against my birthplace, my home, my children." This single individual became the determining factor in the course of the Civil War in Virginia.

Robert E. Lee (1807–1870) shortly before he accepted command of the Virginia forces. Eleanor S. Brockenbrough Library, The Museum of the Confederacy

Two days after leaving the U.S. Army, Lee arrived in Richmond in civilian dress. He had journeyed to the capital at the governor's request to take charge of mobilizing Virginia's military forces. Yet his early labors were many, complicated, and unappreciated.

The raw material for an army was there. Thousands of recruits were marshaling from all over the state, in every type of uniform and sporting every imaginable weapon. From the tidewater came wealthy sons in gaily dressed units; from the hill country came mountaineers in deerskin attire; from campuses marched companies such as the Sons of Liberty and Southern Guard from the University of Virginia and the Liberty Hall Volunteers from Washington College; from the College of William and Mary came President Benjamin Ewell, the professors, and most of the student body.

All echoed the sentiments of one recruit: "Virginia must fight her own battles, defend as best she may her own soil, and so doing defend the whole eastern part of the Confederacy. . . . Noble, grand old state! I love her dearer in her days of tribulation than in her prosperity, and while life is spared me I will fight in her behalf so long as a foe is on her soil."

Lee knew that more practical and immediate problems had to be resolved before fervent volunteers could take to the field. The troops assembling in Richmond had high enthusiasm but little experience. What shoulder arms were available that spring were mostly obsolete flintlock muskets. The number of revolvers and sabers at hand for mounted units was insufficient, cannon were antiquated, ammunition was in short supply. The matériel for war was less than would be required for a large-scale sham battle.

Bringing order out of chaos was Lee's first achievement. He established a basic training camp for infantry at the old fairgrounds on the western edge of Richmond. It appropriately was named Camp Lee. The Richmond College campus became the artillery base of instruction. Smaller training facilities went into operation all over the state. At the same time, Lee summoned a handful of Regular Army officers in Virginia, plus the corps of cadets at the Virginia Military Institute, to act as drill instructors in the Richmond camps.

Slowly, throughout Virginia, 1,000-man regiments evolved from 100-man companies. Antagonisms bred by different economic brackets became less prevalent as social status gave way to military necessity. Men began to look and feel like soldiers. On June 8 Governor Letcher directed that all Virginia forces be transferred into the Confederate army. Lee had done a masterful job. In less than two months, he had organized 40,000 troops, with field and staff officers, and with every regi-

Confederate soldiers arriving in Winchester. *Harper's Weekly*

ment at least partially armed with purchased or confiscated weapons. No one in the Confederacy had done more to prepare for war.

Meanwhile, in Virginia, both North and South gained early martyrs to the cause. Shortly after the state's secession, Federal forces crossed over the Potomac from Washington and occupied Alexandria. Proprietor James W. Jackson of the Marshall House resented their presence. On May 24 he defiantly raised a Confederate flag on the rooftop of his hotel. When New York colonel Elmer Ellsworth personally cut down the standard, Jackson killed Ellsworth on a staircase landing and was himself instantly slain by one of Ellsworth's men.

These were the first two battle deaths of many thousands to come.

The May 24, 1861, encounter between Alexandria tavern proprietor James Jackson and Federal colonel Elmer Ellsworth. *The Soldier in Our Civil War*

. III .

First Battles

L ate in May 1861 Jefferson Davis arrived in Richmond to establish his new presidential headquarters. The refurbished Crenshaw home became the executive mansion for Davis and his family. This handsome structure, a townhouse of three stories and high-ceilinged rooms, stood majestically on a hilltop only three blocks from the Virginia Capitol.

Davis had many admirable qualities: honesty, integrity, high moral standards, military and political experience, genuine love of family, and a soul-deep devotion to the Southern cause. Yet from the outset of his presidency Davis made two major mistakes. First, he chose to be too much a commander in chief and too little the political leader of his country. The Confederacy was blessed at the start with good military commanders; it was badly in need of statesmen. Davis intruded into a crowd and ignored the vacant area where his talents could have been valuable.

The disparity of resources and the facts of geography left the South little choice but to fight a defensive war. Davis initially carried that strategy too far. In his bureaucratic mind, he committed the Confederacy to the traditional departmental system of defense. Troops were to be posted throughout the Confederacy to check the enemy at all points. Any Southern strategy thus became a counteroffensive, a reaction to any Federal move. The problem with such thinking was twofold: the Confederate nation did not have the strength to continue

weathering first blows, and dispersing troops everywhere made concentration anywhere difficult if not impossible. This predicament was not immediately evident
in the first months of war. Few people on either side
expected the contest to last a year. Initial Confederate
successes camouflaged long-range reality.

Four avenues of invasion made Virginia vulnerable
from three different directions. From the northwest,
Federal columns could move eastward across the remote
counties, stream through the mountain passes, and fan
out into the Shenandoah Valley. The northern (or lower)
end of the Valley, opening into Maryland, offered another channel for a Union offensive. From Washington,
troops could move directly southward on Richmond.
Federal forces also could launch an amphibious campaign westward up the wide peninsula of land between
the James and York rivers—a finger of land whose
knuckle was Richmond.

Advances by Federals came early at all points. The
first serious and most far-reaching threat to Virginia
emerged in the western mountains. Its origins were both
internal and external. Virginia's secession did not occur
with statewide support. A long history of grudges and
complaints had set eastern and western Virginia apart.
The mountaineers traditionally looked to the west and
the Ohio River rather than to the east and the Atlantic
seaboard. Western men had little in common with eastern planters, slavery, or the Southern way of life. Therefore, when the Old Dominion withdrew from the Union,
westerners began talking loudly about a withdrawal of
their own.

Federal general George B. McClellan quickly moved
a small army into the mountains. He met with a friendly
reception from citizens. On June 3, in the first land en-

President Jefferson Davis (1808–
1889). *Harper's Pictorial History of
the Great Rebellion*

gagement of the war, McClellan routed a sleeping Confederate camp at Philippi. A month later, while men
cursed the rocky terrain and wet weather, Federals
struck again at Rich Mountain and Carrick's Ford. General Robert S. Garnett, a former commandant at West
Point and a Virginia officer of great promise, was killed
at the latter engagement.

In spite of McClellan's grandiose dispatches to Washington, these clashes were small affairs not pursued to
complete success. However, they did have two wide-

ranging consequences. Now protected by Federal troops, the western Virginians began moving toward independent statehood; and the Union military successes in those first days of war brought McClellan to the attention of Lincoln and his government.

A week after the confrontation at Philippi, a hodgepodge Federal force under Gen. Benjamin F. Butler left Fort Monroe and began moving up the York-James peninsula. On June 10 at Big Bethel—midway between Hampton and Yorktown—Butler's men discovered the 1st North Carolina in their path. The Federals, many in gaudy Zouave uniforms, lost their composure before the fight and began shooting wildly at one another. Exasperated officers finally got them lumbering forward toward the Confederate lines. Two and a half hours of feeble thrusts gained nothing. Butler's command fell back to Fort Monroe. Casualties at Big Bethel were seventy-six Federals and eight Confederates.

Another danger to the state developed at the northern opening of the Shenandoah Valley. Some 18,000 inexperienced Federal militia began concentrating around Harpers Ferry. Their commander was Gen. Robert Patterson, a slow-thinking officer almost as old as the U.S. Constitution. Facing Patterson were Gen. Joseph E. Johnston's 11,000 equally green Southerners.

A cautious advance by Patterson collided on July 5 at Falling Waters with part of the 5th Virginia and one cannon from the Rockbridge Artillery, both Valley units under the immediate command of Gen. Thomas J. Jackson. The skirmish ended largely because of the telling fire of the artillery piece. It was under the direction of an Episcopal priest, Capt. William N. Pendleton. Before sending the first round toward the Federals, Reverend-Captain Pendleton shouted: "The Lord have mercy on their souls! Fire!" After the engagement, and in tribute to their captain, the men of the battery nicknamed their four cannon "Matthew, Mark, Luke, and John."

The fourth Federal offensive baptized Virginia in the blood of a major battle. By early summer the North's largest military force had assembled at Washington: 35,000 untested soldiers under Gen. Irvin McDowell, a Regular Army staff officer who had never commanded in battle. McDowell needed much time to prepare for any kind of offensive. However, pressure from Washington politicians and newspapers forced him to advance his disorganized force into Virginia. His goal was Richmond; but to protect his overland advance, McDowell first had to take control of the railroad junction at Manassas, only thirty miles southwest of the Northern capital.

Confederates were well aware of the importance of the railroads. Waiting at Manassas for McDowell were 22,000 Southern troops. At their head was the "Hero of Fort Sumter," Gen. P. G. T. Beauregard. A graduate of the same West Point class as McDowell, Beauregard had equal parts of intellect, experience, and self-assurance. They were not clearly visible in his small stature, droopy eyes, and bushy mustache.

McDowell's battle plan was to strike Beauregard's force before it could be reinforced by Johnston's troops from Winchester. Patterson's army had the simple responsibility of keeping Johnston pinned in the Valley. Beauregard comprehended Federal intentions as McDowell's huge force approached Manassas. So did Richmond authorities, who instructed Johnston to move his men by rail to Manassas at his discretion.

Johnston made an unobstructed departure from Winchester by having cavalry under Jeb Stuart gallop back

General Pierre G. T. Beauregard
(1818–1893). Eleanor S.
Brockenbrough Library, The
Museum of the Confederacy

and forth in Patterson's front while Southern infantry
headed east. The ruse worked to perfection. By Saturday
evening, July 20, most of Johnston's force was in line
with Beauregard's brigades. Two armed mobs of almost
equal size now stared at each other from opposite banks
of Bull Run. This lazy, shallow stream had steep banks,
a soft bottom, and few places where a large force could
cross easily.

In true mid-nineteenth-century fashion, McDowell
determined to strike Beauregard's left wing with a flank
attack. Beauregard meanwhile had decided on a similar
plan for assaulting the Federals. Thus, when the sun rose
that hot Sabbath of July 21, both armies were leaning
heavily to starboard.

The battle began and lasted as long as it did because
the two forces equally shared inexperience and unpre-

"On the Way to Manassas," sketch by Allen C. Redwood. *Century War Book* (New York, 1894)

paredness. No one on the field was quite sure of what was happening or what to do. Throughout the morning, waves of Federals made disjointed attacks on the Confederate left flank. Near noon, the gray line broke. As Southerners fell back toward a commanding eminence known as Henry House Hill, South Carolina general Barnard Bee looked up and saw massed troops calmly waiting in line on the hilltop.

What Bee shouted to his retreating soldiers has many versions because no one on the field at that chaotic moment wrote it down. Yet most Confederates within hearing recalled Bee as exclaiming: "Look, men! There stands Jackson like a stone wall! Rally around the Vir-

ginians! Let us determine to die here and we will conquer!"

Bee died in the fighting a short while later. Four brigades of Federals swept up Henry House Hill to seize
the crest and victory. Their attack came to an abrupt
halt when Jackson's Virginia regiments, thereafter her-
alded as the "Stonewall Brigade," sent point-blank vol-
leys of musketry into the Union ranks. The hillside
became a huge arena as youths on both sides fought for
hours with the desperation of veterans.

In late afternoon the remaining regiments of Johnston's Valley army arrived on the field. These fresh
troops, as well as some regiments shifted from the Confederate right, slammed into the exposed Federal flank
and swung the battle to the South's favor. What began
as a reasonably orderly Federal retreat became a rout as
thousands of men panicked trying to move down roads
clogged with wagons, caissons, and Washington civilians who had gaily come to Manassas that Sunday to
see the Civil War end. A British reporter contemptuously
described the scene as the "Bull Run Races."

Total losses in the engagement were 847 killed, 2,706
wounded, and 1,325 captured. First Manassas (or First
Bull Run, as Northerners called it) was a small battle by
later Civil War standards. Yet it was the largest and
bloodiest contest in American history up to that time.

More than a fourth of the Confederates on the field
had been Virginians—a fact that caused the state to
grieve the most over its losses. For days after the battle,
trainloads of dead and maimed soldiers arrived in Richmond. The wounded were taken to warehouses, homes,
churches, and other makeshift hospitals for whatever
treatment was available. The slain went to Hollywood
and Oakwood cemeteries. Mournful notes of the "Dead

March" were so constant that a young diarist stated: "It comes and it comes, until I feel inclined to close my eyes and scream."

As far as most Southerners were concerned, the victory at Manassas was the end of the war. Lethargy began to settle over the Confederacy in late summer. The War Department rejected some 260,000 volunteers because there were not arms for them. Most of these men did not volunteer again. The governments of three Southern states refused to contribute arms to the Confederacy on the grounds that their local militia units needed them for each state's protection. South Carolina's governor went one step further: not only did he refuse to send muskets for the army, but after Manassas he asked that some of the weapons already dispatched be returned.

Such complacency was dangerous. Mrs. Mary Chesnut, writing from Richmond at the time, observed: "We will dilly-dally, and Congress orate, and generals parade, until they in the North get up an army three times as large as McDowell's." This prediction was correct. While the South basked in triumph and awaited peace, the North began a serious buildup for prosecution of the struggle. Millions of dollars in orders went to Northern armories and industries; army camps stepped up training schedules; new troops arrived in Washington at the rate of about 5,000 per week that autumn.

The Confederacy and the Union alike had expected to fight the customary war of yesteryear: mass and maneuver, with one grand, climactic battle. What happened along Bull Run prompted a change in Federal thinking. The North in time would usher in tomorrow's war: massive concentrations, hammer blows, constant pressure. The collision at Manassas resembled an engagement in

One of the first drawings of the 1861 battle at Manassas.
Inaccurate in details, it nevertheless underscores the chaos,

suffering, and gallantry exhibited on both sides. *The Soldier in Our Civil War*

the War of 1812, but the siege of Petersburg three years later would bear more resemblance to the wholesale destruction of World War I.

During the lull after Manassas, President Davis sent Lee to the western mountains. The general's assignment was to try and iron out the differences between three brigadiers, each with separate commands and overlapping responsibilities. Two of the generals, Henry A. Wise and John B. Floyd, were former Virginia governors; the third was a professional soldier, William W. Loring. Wise and Floyd disliked each other; Loring, a North Carolinian, resented the presence of two political generals in his area.

Lee was not the man to send into such a situation. He was tactful and solicitous of feelings. What was needed from Richmond was a coldhearted martinet to take firm, complete control of an awkward situation. Lee could not persuade the commanders to move toward necessary unity. Moreover, enemy forces in the area were larger and better organized; what news Lee received was misinformation; rain made roads impassable and campaigning futile. Lee's mission was a failure, and on him fell all the blame. He returned to Richmond looking tired and wearing a beard for the first time.

The western third of the state was lost. In October leading citizens in forty-eight counties determined to secede from Virginia. They accepted the quick support of the Federal government. An area of 24,000 square miles now became a new part of the Union. West Virginia would send 32,000 men into the Federal armies while 8,000 of its sons served in Confederate units, most of them from Virginia.

Other than minor skirmishes between pickets and small cavalry clashes, only one engagement of note occurred in Virginia that fall. A Federal raiding force attempted to cross the Potomac near Leesburg. Confederates under Gen. N. G. ("Shanks") Evans intercepted the probe on high ground overlooking the river. The resulting October 21 battle of Ball's Bluff bordered on a massacre. Many of the 921 Federal losses were soldiers who drowned seeking escape back across the Potomac. Numbered among the dead was Sen. Edward D. Baker of Oregon, a close friend of President Lincoln. Confederate losses in the fighting were 150 men.

High optimism marked the year 1861 in Virginia. With one exception, every Federal invasion of the state had met defeat. The pain of losing the western Virginia counties would not be felt for awhile. In fact, many residents of the tidewater and piedmont felt relief that their cantankerous cousins in the mountains were gone. Christmas in the Confederacy was a joyful occasion. Surely peace would come with the following year.

. IV .

Emergence of a Hero

Genuine grief rolled across the state on January 18 with the news that John Tyler had died in his Richmond hotel room. The former president and longtime Virginia statesman had recently accepted election to the C.S. Congress in yet another public career. Tyler's death severed a strong link with the past. A month later Jefferson Davis stood in pouring rain at the monument to George Washington in Capitol Square and delivered his inaugural address as president of the Confederacy. He emphasized the American ideal that government rests on the consent of the governed. The Confederacy wanted peace, Davis stated, but it would fight with complete determination for independence. In essence, the president repeated his April 1861 statement that all the South asked was "to be left alone."

Such an idea ran counter to the North's avowed aim of preserving the Union. By the first weeks of 1862, the largest army the Western Hemisphere had ever seen stood poised at Washington. Its commander was Gen. George B. McClellan, who had been thrust into high command because of his western Virginia accomplishments. McClellan had serious deficiencies in strategic planning and tactical executions; yet few officers ever displayed greater organizational skills than he in the months after his appointment as general-in-chief of Union forces. McClellan shaped, molded, and polished his Army of the Potomac until it was an awesome mili-

General George B. McClellan (1826–1885). *The Soldier in Our Civil War*

tary machine of some 190,000 well-armed and well-trained men.

The Federal general seems not to have understood that in wartime an army exists to fight. McClellan became too proud of his creation. Preferring grand reviews to combat, he turned a deaf ear to the growing clamor in the North for action. It took a direct order from President Lincoln before McClellan finally took to the field.

His grandiose plan rested on the shaky premises of mass, maneuver, and surprise. Johnston's hopelessly outmanned Confederate forces had spent the winter at Manassas and Centreville. That area, McClellan was convinced, offered too little room for movement. Even if a victory was obtained there, it was too far from the primary goal: Richmond.

Instead, McClellan's final decision was to transport his army on hundreds of boats down the protected supply-line route of the Chesapeake Bay, then attack Richmond head-on from the east by way of the peninsula. The James and York rivers would protect his flanks; both the roads and the countryside would be better for travel. Further, such a move would force Johnston to abandon the Centreville line, thereby easing Confederate pressure on Washington.

As Union preparations for the campaign went forward, North and South made naval history at Hampton Roads. Among the vessels seized by Virginians at Gosport Navy Yard the previous spring was the USS *Merrimack*. Confederate naval personnel spent months converting the wooden cruiser into a revolutionary ironclad battleship. She had a superstructure slanted at a 45-degree angle and guns bristling on every side. The iron plating and heavy armament of the newly christened CSS *Virginia* were expected to compensate for engines so small and rusted that it took the vessel forty minutes to cxccute a 180-degree turn.

On March 8, 1862, the *Virginia* left her Norfolk mooring and lumbered into Hampton Roads in search of battle. Wooden frigates and sloops stationed near Fort Monroe moved to engage the dark, squat ship. Soon a sloop was sinking with guns blazing; a frigate, on fire, ran aground and struck her colors; a second frigate and several other vessels beached to escape from the Confederate warship. The *Virginia* had demonstrated that wood was no defense against iron.

The next day, the *Virginia* crawled back across Hampton Roads to destroy the remainder of the Federal fleet. Unknown to the Confederates, the North too had been constructing an ironclad. The USS *Monitor* was small and agile, with a low superstructure and a revolving turret. Skeptics dismissed the strange-looking vessel as "a tin can on a shingle." She arrived at Hampton Roads just after the *Virginia* scored her first kill.

A new era in naval warfare began when the *Monitor* and *Virginia* met in Norfolk harbor. For two hours the two monsters swapped salvos at close range. Echoes from balls bouncing off iron plating could be heard for miles. The *Virginia* then tried to ram her smaller adversary. When that failed, the Confederate ship swung alongside so that marines could board the *Monitor* and take her with hand-to-hand fighting. The *Monitor* easily slipped astern out of reach. After six hours of combat, the Federal ironclad took cover in shallow water. The battle ended in a draw. Yet every wooden naval vessel in the world was now obsolete.

By April, McClellan had executed the first stage of his offensive. The ponderous Army of the Potomac stood massed in the Yorktown–Fort Monroe area. Johnston, outnumbered by more than two to one, had moved his Confederate army down the peninsula to block McClellan's advance as best he could. With the Union army now at Hampton Roads, Norfolk had to be evacuated. The Confederacy had no choice but to abandon the vital Gosport Navy Yard. Worse from a psychological standpoint, the South gave up the *Virginia*. The ship was not seaworthy enough to venture into the Atlantic Ocean, and the James River was too shallow for the huge vessel to ascend. The *Virginia* was taken a few miles upriver and scuttled.

McClellan's arrival at Yorktown sent apprehension sweeping across Virginia. Panic caused many civilians to

The first duel between ironclads, on March 9, 1862: the *Monitor* (left) and the *Virginia*. *Century War Book*

leave Richmond. A local newspaper warned all readers: "If the Confederacy loses Virginia, it loses the backbone and right arm of the war."

Meanwhile, Davis's military adviser, Gen. Robert E. Lee, moved decisively to counter the threats to the state. He sent a single brigade northward to watch Gen. Irvin McDowell's corps posted at Fredericksburg. Lee beefed up Gen. Stonewall Jackson's force in the Shenandoah

Valley. Then he concentrated everything else he had in order to confront the larger danger of McClellan.

The first half of the Peninsular campaign was not to be the all-out, fully committed battles that would characterize the Civil War two years later. "Little Mac" McClellan and "Uncle Joe" Johnston were two generals lacking in killer instincts. They both were military-wise counterpunchers who preferred to box rather than throw haymakers. Their arena on the peninsula was flat, agriculturally productive country, laced by creeks and country roads; and as one traveled westward, most of the main roadways converged on Richmond.

McClellan's numbers were such that he could have overrun Johnston's position south and west of Yorktown. Yet the Federal commander opted to construct an elaborate system of artillery emplacements from which he could blast the Confederates from his front. "Only McClellan could have hesitated to attack," Johnston sneered. The Confederate commander waited a month while McClellan got his heavy pieces in place, then backed out of artillery range.

Federal forces moved forward cautiously in pursuit. On May 5 portions of the two armies waged a stiff but inconclusive contest in the rain at Williamsburg. Johnston methodically fell back toward Richmond with the hope that some opportunity would arise whereby he could attack part of the mammoth Union army.

McClellan slowly advanced his forces up every road leading to the Confederate capital. His plan was predicated not on fighting alone but on McDowell's 40,000 Federals moving down on Richmond from the north while the Army of the Potomac attacked from the east. With open country in both directions, Richmond seemed to be doomed.

Lincoln, on the other hand, was averse to leaving Washington unguarded. McDowell could join McClellan, he stated, only if Gen. Nathaniel P. Banks's 35,000 Federals in the Shenandoah Valley replaced McDowell at Fredericksburg. McClellan was willing; Banks was willing; McDowell was willing. Stonewall Jackson was not.

Possessed of a fire-and-brimstone Calvinism which

General Joseph E. Johnston (1807–1891). The Museum of the Confederacy, courtesy of the National Archives

made him pray hard and fight hard, Jackson was a man whose eccentricities were viewed as simply part of a hidden genius. He had no intention of being a bystander to Federal strategy. Two facts were clear to the Confederate commander in the Valley that spring: he had to protect his beloved Shenandoah and its immense agricultural produce from enemy destruction, and he had to prevent Federal concentration in front of Richmond.

Jackson had passed the winter in Winchester, a proud, old town where George Washington had headquartered during the French and Indian War. Winchester was the key to the Shenandoah Valley, a 165-mile corridor between the two easternmost ranges of the Alleghenies. The 1862 Valley campaign that "Old Jack" unleashed was one of the most sterling movements in all of military history. It was tailor-made for Jackson's greatest talents: independence of command, wide latitude for action, rapid and secret marches against a hopelessly divided opponent.

On March 11 Jackson abandoned Winchester and retreated southward up the Shenandoah to Mount Jackson. His ever-vigilant cavalry chief, Col. Turner Ashby, reported ten days later that elements of Banks's Federal army were moving east out of the Valley. Jackson led his troops on an unbroken thirty-seven-mile march and struck part of Banks's force at Kernstown, just south of Winchester.

Jackson had expected to hit only the rear guard of the Federal army. Too little intelligence and too much initia-

General Richard S. Ewell (1817–1872). *Harper's Pictorial History of the Great Rebellion*

tive produced a setback. The March 23 attack at Kernstown found Jackson's small force engaging a full Federal division. Southern attacks through the afternoon met with defeat. Yet Jackson accomplished a major objective in that two Federal divisions en route to Fredericksburg were ordered back to the Valley. Some 3,600 Confederates had immobilized ten times their number.

For a month Jackson rested his little band at Elk Run and awaited the chance to strike again. It came in late April when he received a division of troops under Gen. Richard S. Ewell. A sound soldier who loved combat, Ewell hardly looked the part. "Baldy Dick" had a shining pate and a constant look of surprise. A high-pitched voice and bulging eyes that always fixed a person with a baleful direct gaze added to his oddities.

The Confederate force in the Valley numbered 17,000 soldiers. On the day that Johnston abandoned the Yorktown line, Jackson went into action. He left Ewell to watch Banks's army, which had advanced to Harrisonburg. Jackson moved by a secret, 270-degree route to Staunton. From there he crossed a mountain range and on May 8 defeated part of Gen. John C. Frémont's army moving in from the west. Jackson's succinct victory dispatch ("God blessed our arms with victory at McDowell yesterday") sent Confederate officials scurrying for maps to ascertain the general's whereabouts.

Jackson's game of hide-and-seek had merely begun. Informants such as teenaged Belle Boyd kept him fully informed of Federal dispositions. The Confederates now started north, veered to the east across Massanutten Mountain, then turned north on the blind side of the Massanutten that divided the Valley between Harrisonburg and Strasburg. Banks suddenly discovered that Jackson was not retreating, as he had supposed; Jackson's army had overrun a Federal garrison at Front Royal and was in Banks's rear.

A wild race ensued for Winchester. Banks left the Valley Turnpike (now U.S. 11) cluttered with discarded wagons and equipment. He reached Winchester just before Jackson delivered a May 25 attack which sent the Federal army racing toward the Potomac River. "Stop, soldier! Don't you love your country?" Banks reportedly shouted to one of his fleeing men. "Yes!" the soldier replied without breaking his stride, "and I'm trying to get back to it as fast as I can!"

Alarmed officials in Washington moved promptly to stop the actions of that "Rebel upstart" in the Valley. Banks was of no help: his troops were scattered and, by the general's admission, "not in condition to move with promptitude." Nevertheless, Federal officials designed a huge vise to entrap Jackson. Two divisions of McDowell's corps marched westward from Fredericksburg while Frémont's command pushed eastward through the mountains. In all, 50,000 Federals were moving to encircle an army barely a third of their combined numbers.

Jackson escaped the trap by marching hard. His Stonewall Brigade tramped fifty-two miles in thirty-six hours through a driving rain and without food. The Confederates reached Harrisonburg and rested while Jackson watched Federal columns pursuing him on either side of the Massanutten. Jackson moved to the southeast of Harrisonburg, divided his forces, and lashed out at the two wings. Ewell easily blunted Frémont's probes on June 8 at Cross Keys. The following day, in the hardest fighting of the campaign, Jackson's attacks at Port Republic against Gen. James Shields's troops overran the other Federal wing. Union forces sol-

General Thomas J. ("Stonewall") Jackson (1824–1863). The Museum of the Confederacy, courtesy of the National Archives

emnly marched down the Valley in retreat. The great campaign was over.

What Jackson had done was truly remarkable. He kept a potential force of 175,000 Federals from joining in a fatal encirclement of Richmond. In one month of campaigning (May 4–June 9), Jackson had checked Frémont's army threatening Staunton; he had chased Banks from Virginia for a period; he had kept McDowell's corps pinned at Fredericksburg. The trio of Federal commanders not only had failed to crush Jackson but had been defeated in turn and would never regain lost esteem.

In the forty-eight days beginning with the advance to Kernstown, the largely inexperienced Confederate army had marched 676 miles—an average of fourteen miles for each day of the campaign. Jackson's "foot cavalry" had fought five battles and six skirmishes and had brushed with the enemy almost daily for a month. Confederates had killed or wounded 3,500 Federals, taken another 3,500 as prisoners, and seized 10,000 muskets, 9 cannon, and tons of badly needed supplies. Jackson's losses seemed slight in comparison: 3,000 men killed, wounded, and missing, plus 3 guns. Overnight, with public acclaim and confidence, the South elevated Stonewall Jackson to the pinnacle of Confederate popularity.

Widespread reports that the eccentric Jackson was actually insane caused the Richmond *Whig* to chortle on June 12 that "a liberal reward will be given for the apprehension of a confirmed lunatic, named Old Stonewall, who escaped from the Asylum, in this place, early in the Spring" and had been bedeviling Yankees ever since.

As Jackson was winning fame in the Valley, Confederate officials at Richmond were preparing for the worst. McClellan's army continued to approach the capital. Women and children left Richmond for havens elsewhere. Government records were packed for transfer to a safer place. Millions of dollars' worth of tobacco was made ready for the torch. Every available Confederate unit in the area rushed to strengthen Johnston's retreating army. Richmond braced for battle—and a dark future.

. V .

Lee Takes Command

Rain fell on Virginia every day in May 1862, and the weather had a direct effect in bringing McClellan's grand offensive against Richmond to a halt. Johnston's Confederates had retired slowly in the face of the gigantic Union army. The daily downpours and depthless mud, but especially McClellan's indecisiveness, so impaired the invasion that in twenty-six days the Army of the Potomac marched less than forty miles.

The James River was navigable all the way to the fall line at Richmond. Federal gunboats steamed upriver alongside McClellan's left without encountering opposition. On May 15 the Union vessels reached Drewry's Bluff. The 200-foot cliff not only stood at a bend in the James; its several rifled cannon also commanded a long stretch of the river. An artillery duel of three and a half hours ensued before the Federal ships gave up the fight and slipped downriver. One of the vessels driven back was the supposedly invincible ironclad *Monitor*.

By the last week of May, McClellan's army had reached the hamlet of Seven Pines. Church steeples in Richmond were visible only eight miles away. One mighty surge by the Federals, and the Confederacy's principal city would fall. McClellan had no thought of attack. He had encountered an obstacle neglected on most maps of that time. Meandering diagonally across the peninsula was an odd stream known as the Chickahominy River. It had no banks. Spongy land spread out on either side, and how wide the river was depended on

Drewry's Bluff on the James River, seven miles from Richmond. Oil on canvas, by John Ross Key. The Museum of the Confederacy

when last it had rained. By the end of May, the Chicka-hominy was such a broadly flowing swamp that it split the Federal army almost in half and severed most communications between the two wings. McClellan halted his divided army while he contemplated the next move.

This was the moment that Uncle Joe Johnston had long been seeking. He quickly massed troops in front of McClellan's smaller force on the south side of the Chick-ahominy. On May 31 Confederates attacked at Seven

Pines. Confused fighting raged for two days through rain-soaked woods and in fields that resembled lakes. Many wounded men who slumped to the ground disappeared in water.

For the Confederates, it was a case of good plans badly executed. Surprise attacks lacked punching power; Federals were content to stay on the defensive behind strong earthworks until reinforcements arrived and threatened the Confederate flank. Neither North nor South gained anything of significance as casualties surpassed those incurred at First Manassas.

Seven Pines nevertheless had major consequences for both sides. McClellan surveyed the carnage on the battlefield and resolved to avoid such combat again. He settled down to await better weather and to complete what he enigmatically termed "necessary preliminaries." Johnston had been wounded in the first day's action and would be incapacitated for months. President Davis bypassed all of his field commanders and named Gen. Robert E. Lee to lead the Confederate defensive force.

Lee's problems on assuming command were many and critical. Richmond had some defenses but nothing that could withstand an assault by the powerful Federal army. Lee himself had not been under fire so far in the Civil War, and he had never commanded anything larger than a regiment. Now he was at the head of the largest Confederate force in the field. Worse, the Army of Northern Virginia looking to him for direction was not an army. It was a huge assemblage of brigades and divisions, with poor organization, some inept officers, and practically no battle experience.

An indefatigable Lee spent the next three weeks working almost around the clock. His military talents blossomed. While his field experience was limited, Lee had learned much about army command from Mexican War service on Gen. Winfield Scott's staff. Lee was also brilliant in the art of field fortifications. He assigned able-bodied civilians as well as soldiers to construct a system of strong earthworks on the east and north sides of Richmond.

Lee meanwhile collected available units, rebuilt a command network, shuffled officers here and there, and tightened efficiency at every level in the ranks of his army. The Confederates were in need of everything; but unlike McClellan, Lee had no thoughts of passing the time in polishing his creation. He was determined, once the situation was reasonably secure, to launch a counteroffensive against the huge enemy force poised a few miles away.

The Chickahominy still flowed through McClellan's army. On the western face of the river was the main body of the Federals. The right wing was behind the stream in expectation of joining hands at any time with McDowell's corps coming down from Fredericksburg. Lee's plan was to assail that isolated Union right with everything he had. Once he caved in the flank, Lee hoped for an envelopment of McClellan's army which would pressure the larger force into defeat or surrender.

To execute so daring a movement, Lee first had to locate McClellan's right flank. Lee dispatched his cavalry chief, the colorfully dressed and adventurous Jeb Stuart, with 1,200 horsemen on a heavy reconnaissance. Stuart headed north on June 12 as if riding to join Jackson in the Valley. Beyond Ashland, the Confederate cavalry veered east and galloped toward the enemy lines.

Stuart found the end of the Federal position with little effort. With a combination of logic and daring, the ever-dashing Stuart concluded that it would be too dangerous to retrace his route back to Lee. He thereupon rode across the Union lines of communication and across the peninsula itself. On at least one occasion he skirmished with Federal cavalry under the command of his father-in-law, Gen. Philip St. George Cooke. The 100-mile ride took Stuart completely around McClellan's 100,000 soldiers. On June 15 the cavalry detachment returned triumphantly to Richmond with 165 prisoners and 260 captured animals—all at a loss of one officer killed.

The "Ride around McClellan" contained more excitement than strategic gain. Stuart's feat put McClellan on guard. Yet it also made the Yankee army appear less ominous, and it made Jeb Stuart a household name thereafter. Coming on the heels of Jackson's brilliant success in the Shenandoah, the foray sent Confederate morale soaring. A War Department clerk in Richmond exclaimed: "What a change! No one dreams of the loss of the capital!"

Barely three weeks after assuming command of the Southern army, Lee began his counteroffensive. It became known as the Seven Days' campaign. Leaving a skeletal force under generals John B. Magruder and Benjamin Huger to demonstrate between McClellan and Richmond, Lee had secretly transferred the bulk of his army to Mechanicsville and the Federal right. Jackson had departed the Valley with his forces and was moving in to attack simultaneously with Lee. The campaign that followed was an astonishing reversal of the military situation at Richmond. Yet nothing went right for the Confederates on any day of the fighting.

Jackson did not arrive on the field as expected on the twenty-sixth. General A. P. Hill on his own initiative opened the battle by sending his division against a Federal corps entrenched on a rise behind boggy Beaver Dam Creek. Sheets of Union cannon fire and musketry raked Southern lines and covered the muddy ground with dead and maimed soldiers. Hill took 1,500 casualties while his adversary, Gen. Fitz-John Porter, reported the loss of only 360 men.

During the night Porter withdrew four miles southward to a new position east of Gaines' Mill. Lee resumed the attacks the next day. The divisions of Hill and Gen. James Longstreet assailed the Federal lines while

General James E. B. ("Jeb") Stuart
(1833–1864). *Century War Book*

the whole Confederate army anxiously looked for the still-tardy Jackson to attack on the left. Again Federal fire chewed holes in Lee's ranks. The usually gruff Longstreet stated of Gaines' Mill: "There was more individual gallantry displayed upon this field than any I have ever seen."

The battle had raged for six hours when Jackson's troops finally entered the action. Weight of Confederate numbers and exhaustion caused the Federal line to crumple. Porter retreated southward after nightfall. Lee had won his first victory, but at the staggering cost of almost 9,000 men, including two generals badly wounded and ten regimental colonels slain.

Lee drove hard on McClellan's flanks as the Union commander sought to effect a "change of base" from White House Landing on the Pamunkey River to Harrison's Landing on the James. Southbound roads became clogged with 100,000 Federals, 4,000 wagons, and 350 guns all trying to reach safety. Lee just as desperately was trying to deliver a deathblow.

Fighting on June 29 at Savage Station proved a missed opportunity for the Confederates, whose attacks were too little and too late. The next day Hill and Longstreet swerved in from the west and struck McClellan's columns at Frayser's Farm (or Glendale, as it is sometimes called). Jackson's failure to lend support from his White Oak Swamp position on the other side of the Federals left Hill and Longstreet alone to attack parts of five Union divisions. The Confederates inflicted more losses than they suffered—over 5,000 casualties occurred in this little-known engagement—but the Southern forces gained no tactical advantage.

That night Lee got the separated parts of his army together while McClellan concentrated his forces near the James. The main Federal line was on a 150-foot-high slope known as Malvern Hill. It was a mile long, flanked by deep gullies and facing a broad open expanse. McClellan placed over 200 guns on the hill and packed infantrymen around them.

An enormous amount of supplies and equipment discarded by the retreating Federals convinced Lee that one more battle would overpower "those people," as he customarily termed his opponents. On July 1 Lee sent lines of Confederates forward in an attack on Malvern Hill. Massed Union cannon, armed with double loads of canister and with a clear field of fire, tore apart one of the most heroic charges of the war. Some 5,000 Confederates fell in the brief battle. "It was not war," a North Carolina general commented; "it was murder."

McClellan then could have utilized Federal numbers and Confederate instability to make a successful counterthrust of his own. Instead, he withdrew to Harrison's Landing and encamped in the mud. His campaign to seize Richmond had collapsed ingloriously.

The results of the Seven Days foretold much about the future. McClellan had lost only one engagement. His 16,500 casualties represented barely 10 percent of his command, while Lee's 20,000 losses comprised about a fourth of the Confederate army. What McClellan had lost even more painfully for the Union cause was his initiative. His thoughts of taking Richmond had shifted to saving his army.

Lee, in contrast, had bloodied the Army of the Potomac and seriously damaged its self-confidence. In the process his troops had seized 52 Federal cannon and 30,000 shoulder arms. Most importantly, Lee had brought boldness and leadership to a force which only weeks earlier was disorganized and searching for a reputation. He also had begun to instill his soldiers with a newfound sense of invincibility which would make them a far stronger military machine than the sum of their parts.

In terms of human payment for the success, though, the cost had been severe. The fighting from Seven Pines through Malvern Hill sent 21,000 wounded Confederates streaming into Richmond. Maimed soldiers arrived in wagonloads; hundreds of others stumbled along the streets in search of help. Chimborazo and Winder military hospitals, both barely completed, went into full operation. Churches, warehouses, business shops, and scores of private homes all became treatment centers as

The Confederate attack at Malvern Hill, an old-fashioned, straight-ahead assault against a strong, fixed position. *The Soldier in Our Civil War*

Townspeople tending wounded soldiers in Richmond during June
1862. *Century War Book*

untold numbers of Richmonders extended helping
hands to their bleeding defenders. A resident of the capital sighed: "We live in one immense hospital, and
breathe the vapors of the charnel house."

The Confederate army had little time to straighten its
ranks or enjoy its laurels. By mid-July another thrust on
Virginia was under way. Federal general John Pope was
a loudmouthed braggart who came from the West with
a modest reputation. Lincoln placed him in command of
the new Army of Virginia—70,000 soldiers formerly in
the commands of Banks, McDowell, and Frémont. The

Union president then ordered Pope southward into the Virginia piedmont to threaten Richmond from the north. Pope sought to inspire his new troops with a series of morale-building pronouncements. Instead, his statements were bumbling and insulting condemnations of eastern soldiers. "Let us look before us and not behind," Pope asserted.

This new army leader brought something besides pomposity to the Civil War in Virginia. He was going to wage war against civilians. Living off the country would be Pope's policy. Food and property of any resident in his path were subject to seizure. When resistance was encountered, homes would be burned. Not only that, but civilians of any age would be executed if any Federal troops were shot by what Pope called "bushwhackers."

General John Pope (1822–1872).
The Soldier in Our Civil War

The Union general made no attempt to conceal his pleasure at implementing such tactics.

Pope's campaign began to turn northern Virginia counties into a vast wasteland. Across the state, citizens voiced outrage at such military behavior. Pope became the Federal general for whom Lee had the most intense dislike. "That man" must be "suppressed," Lee stated.

With the same assurance that McClellan had exhibited in 1861, Pope led his army from northern Virginia into the rolling piedmont country to the south. His target was the strategic railroad junction at Gordonsville. By the second week of August, the Federals had occupied Culpeper between the Rappahannock and Rapidan rivers.

What the Federal commander underestimated from first to last was the audacity of his opponent. As Pope led his army into the piedmont, Lee concluded that McClellan's offensive spirit was spent. Unhesitatingly, Lee sent Jackson's part of the army to Gordonsville to impede Pope's advance. The rest of the Southern army would hold McClellan at bay for a while longer.

On August 9, after advancing from the rail junction, Jackson struck the van of Pope's forces south of Culpeper at Cedar Mountain. The Federals were Gen. Nathaniel Banks's veterans from the Valley campaign. Both sides delivered heavy assaults during the afternoon contest. Federals were close to turning Jackson's left when a combination of Jackson personally rallying his men and the timely arrival of A. P. Hill's six-brigade "Light Division" sent Banks's brigades limping from the field.

McClellan, meanwhile and reluctantly, was abandoning the peninsula. This Union withdrawal from eastern Virginia left Lee free to give undivided attention to Pope in northern Virginia. The Confederate commander uti lized the advantage of inner lines of defense to shift the main part of his army quickly by rail to Gordonsville. Lee reunited with Jackson while McClellan, slowly returning to Washington with his army, was under orders to send pieces of it to Pope's aid.

It was imperative for Lee to deal with Pope before McClellan appeared with the whole Army of the Potomac. The Confederate need to reoccupy northern Virginia was likewise acute. Lee thereupon devised a bold plan for eliminating Pope's presence. His strategy was to ignore the traditional wisdom of concentrating in the face of the enemy. Rather, Lee once more would divide his smaller army.

He, with Longstreet's troops, would hold Pope along the Rappahannock line. Jackson and his 24,000 "foot cavalry" would make a secret and rapid march around the western flank of the sprawling Federal forces and strike for Pope's rear—specifically the Union supply depot at Manassas Junction. Lee would then close his forces, with Pope in the middle, and go for the kill.

Early on August 25 Jackson's troops marched away. They carried only muskets, ammunition, and skimpy rations stuffed in their pockets. Hardened troops who took pride in their hardness tramped fifty miles in two days. They trekked northwestward, then turned east and crossed Bull Run Mountains. Late on the twenty-sixth, Jackson struck the Orange and Alexandria Railroad at Bristoe Station. He was behind Pope. Eight miles down the track lay Manassas Junction.

Confederates reached Pope's supply base the following afternoon. For the impoverished Rebels, it was Christmas in August. Warehouses were crammed to the ceiling, two miles of loaded freight cars stood on sidings, packed barrels and boxes were stacked along the tracks, and more ammunition lay for the taking than the Confederacy could produce in a year.

Soldiers who had subsisted for days on green corn and unripened apples enjoyed a copious feast. After that, they gathered everything they could carry, set fire to the rest, and disappeared anew. A now-enraged Pope convinced himself that Jackson was running for his life. The Federal general spread out his army in posse-fashion and began backtracking to the north. Unshaken by the masses of Federals moving toward him, Jackson carefully selected a battleground of his own choosing and waited.

On August 28 Jackson ambushed a portion of the Union army as it marched casually along the Warrenton Turnpike (now U.S. 29). The suddenness and intensity of Jackson's assault at Groveton caught the Federals off guard. They recovered quickly; and in a fierce firefight, Pope's men displayed more determination than their general had shown in the campaign. Both sides gave and received heavy losses. One of Jackson's ablest lieutenants, Gen. Richard Ewell, lost a leg in the action.

Pope still felt that Jackson was retreating. He excitedly spent the early part of the following day marching and countermarching his troops in search of the elusive Confederate. Pope soon reached the edge of the old Manassas battlefield. There he found Jackson's forces entrenched in and on either side of an unfinished railroad cut. The Federal commander now substituted rashness for boastfulness. Pope was so anxious to destroy Jackson that he could not wait for his scattered units to consolidate. Oblivious to warnings from his officers, Pope on August 29 hurled divisions in piecemeal fashion against Jackson's strong earthworks. The fox now had a chance to lash out at the hounds.

Lines of Federals made six costly attacks. The Confederates repulsed each one. Pope continued the assaults the next day. Jackson's line held, although at one point Confederates who had exhausted their ammunition threw rocks at the charging Yankees. Pope's mania to neutralize Jackson once and for all blinded him to everything else.

Suddenly, disaster struck the Federal army. Longstreet's brigades—basically the other half of Lee's army—arrived on Pope's left flank after a hard march across the mountains. These 30,000 fresh Confederates struck the exposed Federal flank like an avalanche. One Billy Yank in the battle described Longstreet's entrance into the contest as being "like demons emerging from the earth . . . mad with excitement, rage, and the fearful desire for blood."

Heavy artillery fire supported the soldiers of Longstreet and Jackson as they surged forward with cheers. Pope's line bent, and bent some more, as Federals found themselves all but overwhelmed. By nightfall Pope's defeated army was plodding through a steady rain toward Washington. The two sides at Second Manassas had been about equal in strength. Confederate victory came at a cost of 9,200 men, while Pope suffered 16,000 losses.

Lee made one last effort to "suppress" Pope for good. Again he sent Jackson on a sweeping northeast march around the Federal right. Weary Rebels trudged through darkness and rainfall before striking part of Pope's forces at Chantilly (near present Dulles Airport). Federals managed to beat back the attacks but in the process lost two accomplished generals, Philip Kearny and Isaac I. Stevens. Pope's month-long campaign had accomplished nothing but lengthier casualty lists. Some of the

Confederates out of ammunition hurling stones during the August
30 fighting at Second Manassas. *Century War Book*

blame for the Union failure rested on McClellan. He had shown no inclination to assist Pope, whom he disliked, in a battle which McClellan did not want.

History probably contains no parallel to what Lee did in those summer months of 1862. On June 1 he had taken command of a disjointed army driven to the outskirts of Richmond by the largest military force ever seen in North America; if the capital fell, the Southern hopes for independence would be gone. Now, a mere ninety days later, Lee had whipped the general facing him, had whipped another general approaching from a different direction, and had transferred the Civil War from the neighborhood of Richmond to the environs of Washington. Pope was hiding in Washington, McClellan was reduced to thinking of defense, Virginia was free of any threatening Union forces, and Lee now was making plans to strike into the North. It was a complete turnabout—from imminent defeat to possible victory—and it had all happened in three short months.

. VI .

Exchanging Defeats

Lee's decision to carry the war into the North seems foolhardy in retrospect. Yet the other options available to him were more dangerous. The Army of Northern Virginia was in bad condition. Confederates still in the ranks after four months of intense campaigning were tired. Most of them lacked shoes, and all were in tatters. Horses were barely fit to drag cannon. Wagons creaked from overuse. Lee had 53,000 troops at hand, but McClellan theoretically could bring three times that number to bear. For Lee to sit and do nothing was to ask for annihilation.

Withdrawing toward Richmond would reopen the northern piedmont to another Federal invasion and further destruction. Virginia farmers also needed an undisturbed opportunity to gather the summer's meager crops. A Southern offensive might persuade Maryland to join the Confederacy, thereby surrounding the Northern capital with hostile territory. If Lee's offensive proved successful, the campaign might reap the greater dividend of securing needed recognition and assistance from England, France, or both. Best of all, Lee's drive might shatter Northern insistence on reunion and bring peace.

The potentialities for the Confederacy were so grand. That is why Antietam Creek was so devastating.

A woman in Leesburg early in September watched the long Southern columns heading toward the Potomac. "The Lord bless your dirty, ragged souls!" she shouted

in tribute. Western Marylanders were not so receptive, and McClellan—now back in command of the eastern Union armies—had left Washington in pursuit. Lee had to pause at Frederick to study his maps for the next move.

With no means of supply, Lee actually was conducting a raid in force rather than a prolonged invasion. Thus, what dictated the next move depended on what the last move had accomplished. Lee saw that Frederick was the apex of a triangle, with Hagerstown to the west across

Lee's army, summer of 1862, showing wear and tear but filled with determination and confidence. *Century War Book*

a range of mountains and Federal-held Harpers Ferry to the southwest. The Confederate general then made a fateful decision: even though in enemy territory, he would divide his small army into three parts.

Jackson and the largest contingent would curl back to seize Harpers Ferry and clear an escape route into the Shenandoah Valley. A Confederate division was sent back to approach Harpers Ferry from the southeast. Longstreet would march over to Hagerstown and await Jackson's return. Once Jackson rejoined the army, Lee would use the mountains as a screen and resume the advance on Pennsylvania.

These movements had been under way for only two days when the Federal army reached Frederick and the abandoned Confederate campsites. An Indiana soldier chanced upon a copy of the orders detailing Lee's lines of march. McClellan thus became beneficiary of one of the greatest leaks in American military history. His outnumbered adversary was divided into three pieces, and the Union army was closer to the segments than they were to each other. The entire campaign hinged now on McClellan's boldness.

Demons of self-doubt and uncertainty inside the Federal general sprouted again. McClellan had over 80,000 troops immediately at hand. Yet he estimated Lee's strength at 120,000 soldiers (two and half times the actual number). So McClellan inched forward ever so slowly in search of his foe.

At South Mountain, on September 14, D. H. Hill's troops stood off attacks from five Federal divisions. It was one of the great defensive battles of the war. Harvey Hill's division took a frightful pounding before withdrawing under cover of darkness, but it bought Lee a day to consolidate his army. Jackson seized Harpers Ferry and its 12,000 defenders the next day. The quick-marching Stonewall left A. P. Hill's division to secure the post before hastening north to reunite with Lee. To expedite the junction, Lee shifted his forces southward twelve miles from Hagerstown to Sharpsburg. The village was a more central location for Lee, and it was closer to the natural defense line of the Potomac River.

McClellan in the meantime watched all of Lee's movements from atop battle-scarred South Mountain. Lee carefully placed the 45,000 troops he had along the dips and swells of the high ground overlooking Antietam Creek. Almost twice as many Federals slowly moved into battle line. The stage was set for another Lee-McClellan confrontation.

Never in its gallant history did the Army of Northern Virginia endure such a day as Wednesday, September 17, 1862. It was the bloodiest one-day battle in the nation's history. McClellan chose not to use his great strength of numbers in a massive assault at all points. Instead, he sent corps and divisions into battle first on Lee's left, then into the Confederate center, and finally against the Southern right. Lee again used inner lines of defense skillfully.

Hour after hour, across open ground, through crop-covered fields, up and down ridges, soldiers blue and gray struggled back and forth in combat that at times resembled huge waves crashing against rocks and at other times was a wild melee of hand-to-hand combat. Place-names such as the East Wood, West Wood, Dunkard Church, Bloody Lane, and Burnside's Bridge became unforgettable symbols of sacrifice. Units melted away under the withering fire; dead attackers and defenders were found in rows where they fell; the smoke, and confusion, and the screams of the dying turned the normally peaceful countryside into a living hell.

A Federal assault in midafternoon was on the verge of breaking Lee's right and severing his escape route. At that critical moment, A. P. Hill's division ran onto the field from Harpers Ferry and smashed into the Federal left. This timely arrival by the Culpeper general saved Lee's army. Nightfall brought the battle to a merciful end. The bloodshed of that day at Antietam Creek was appalling. Total casualties were 23,110 men, including over 6,000 dead and dying. By comparison, D-Day in

General A. Powell Hill (1825–
1865). National Archives

General Ambrose E. Burnside
(1824–1881). *Century War Book*

World War II produced only a fourth of those losses among American troops.

With one of every three of his soldiers killed or injured, Lee had no choice but to return home. The daring stroke on behalf of Southern independence had been blunted. Vastly outnumbered in both men and supplies, Lee could hope only to outlast his enemy's determination to conquer Virginia.

The Army of Northern Virginia halted at Winchester for six weeks of recuperation. McClellan's Army of the Potomac encamped at Harpers Ferry, twenty miles away. Lee used this time to reorganize his army into two equal segments: the First Corps under "my old war horse," as Lee affectionately called South Carolina–born James Longstreet, and the Second Corps under the humorless but ingenious Jackson.

McClellan continued his habit of using "needed reorganization" as an excuse for not doing battle. Lincoln demanded that the Union army move forward. McClellan did so—at so cautious a pace that Lincoln's patience finally snapped. On November 5 the president removed McClellan from command of the army he had created and appointed Gen. Ambrose E. Burnside in his stead.

Burnside was Regular Army, honest and likable, with huge muttonchop whiskers that allegedly popularized the word "sideburns." He had many good qualities. Commanding an army was not one of them, as Burnside himself freely admitted. Yet one cannot fault him for trying. Burnside knew that the North clamored for a quick end to the war. The battle scheme he developed was excellent on paper. It might well have succeeded if Burnside had been able to compensate when plans went awry.

His strategy was to shift the Union army quickly from Lee's front in the piedmont, move east and cross the Rappahannock River at Fredericksburg. This would put him between Lee and Richmond. All went well at first as Burnside actually stole a march on Lee. The Army of the Potomac reached the heights across the river from Fredericksburg and found only a token force of Rebels in its front. Yet the pontoon bridges on which Burnside's forces were to cross the Rappahannock were not there. This logistical foul-up in Washington brought the advance through Virginia to an abrupt stop. Burnside sat down to await the arrival of the pontoons.

By the time they were at hand, so was Lee's army. Fredericksburg lay close along the riverbank. Burnside's army was massed on Stafford Heights directly across the Rappahannock from the city. Obviously Lee could not make a stand inside the picturesque colonial town. However, from the river Fredericksburg stretched back on flat and open country for one to two miles before reaching high ground extending parallel to the river some seven miles. The ridge immediately behind Fredericksburg was known as Marye's Heights. At its base was a breast-high stone wall which marked the path of a sunken road.

Lee carefully positioned his army in the road and all along the high ground behind it. Longstreet commanded the left, which was closest to Fredericksburg. Jackson held the right and enjoyed a two-mile open plain between his woodland entrenchments and the river. Despite the unusually long battle line, Lee was able to pack it with 78,000 Confederate infantry and 300 guns.

With his original plan of outflanking Lee no longer practicable, Burnside should have backed off and pursued other options. Such a deviation was not in Burnside's makeup. This simple commander made a simple decision. He would do with the Army of the Potomac what McClellan would not do: attack straight ahead in force. The fact that Lee's army was at peak strength and was waiting for him in a near-perfect defensive position seems not to have bothered Burnside in the least.

On December 11, with the pontoons finally at hand, Burnside sought to bridge the river. A brigade of Mississippi sharpshooters concealed in buildings picked off the Federal engineers one by one. Over 100 Union cannon along Stafford Heights then bombarded Fredericksburg at point-blank range. Buildings collapsed or were blown apart; a pall of smoke swirled upward in the wintry air. Federals in force crossed the Rappahannock and occupied the battered town. What followed was so unlike the Army of the Potomac. Yankees indiscriminately looted shops and homes. Perhaps it was frustration over the campaign, or possibly many of those soldiers smelled death on the morrow.

Saturday, December 13, dawned cold and foggy. In midmorning the sun popped through and battle exploded. The first major action occurred on Lee's right in Jackson's sector. A Federal division under Gen. George G. Meade started across the lowlands. Its progress was impeded for a period by enfilading fire from two cannon under the command of youthful Maj. John Pelham. Meade's determined soldiers renewed their charge, slammed into the woods where Confederates were firing rapidly, and momentarily pierced Jackson's line. Musketry from three sides and Southern reinforcements pouring into the sector routed the Federals and sent the survivors scurrying back to safety.

Around noon, the Union effort switched from Jackson's front to that of Longstreet at Marye's Heights. Out

Drawing of one of the futile Union attacks against Marye's Heights at Fredericksburg. *Harper's Weekly*

of Fredericksburg thousands of Federals moved with parade-ground precision. Bands played, flags arched in the sky, and Union columns marched in cadence as they started toward the hill 400 yards away. Lee's men calmly waited for the command to open fire. When it came, Marye's Heights seemed to explode in flames of musket fire and artillery salvos.

The Federal attacks were as heroic as they were hopeless. Brigade after brigade of Union soldiers advanced steadily into the constant leaden storm. They fell in such piles that other charging units had difficulty getting over and around fallen comrades. Fourteen assaults were made on Marye's Heights and the sunken road. No Federal soldier got within fifty yards of the Confederate position. A Union private in the battle stated of his compatriots: "They reach a point within a stone's throw of the stone wall . . . that terrible stone wall. No farther. They try to go beyond but are slaughtered. Nothing could advance farther and live."

At one point in the lopsided contest, Lee turned to Longstreet. "It is well that war is so terrible," he said. Otherwise, "we should grow too fond of it."

Darkness ended the killing. Burnside's debacle at Fredericksburg cost him 12,600 soldiers—a figure about equal to Federal casualties at Antietam Creek. Lee's dead and wounded were little more than a third of that number. London newspaperman Frank Lawley described the battlefield a day or so later. "There, in every attitude of death, lying so close to each other that you might step from body to body, lay acres of the Federal dead. . . . By universal consent of those who have seen all the great battles of this war, nothing like it has ever been seen before."

Something worse than defeat permeated the Union army. It was demoralization. Four generals openly called for Burnside's removal. Union soldiers began deserting at the rate of 100 per day. On January 20, 1863, Burnside sought redemption by trying to take his army across the Rappahannock several miles upriver from Fredericksburg. The weather turned miserable. Burnside watched his men struggle in rain and mire for two days before abandoning what newspapers derided as the "Mud March." Thoroughly disgraced by then, Burnside must have felt a sense of liberation when Lincoln removed him from command.

Both sides then settled into winter quarters on opposite banks of the Rappahannock. Severe weather, swollen streams, and unserviceable roads blocked all military movements. Confederates found solace in the first of two religious revivals that swept through the Army of Northern Virginia. Federals huddled around campfires and speculated over who next would lead them, and to where.

Events in 1862 had obliterated the early glamor and excitement of war. A long, grinding, incalculably bloody struggle had replaced illusions of a quick and not-too-painless contest. Each side had made invasions of the other's territory and had failed. The Confederates had scored dramatic triumphs but they had come at a frightening cost of life. Northern commanders had fumbled great opportunities and were left with only the knowledge that the men in the ranks were better than the generals who led them.

While the Civil War in Virginia now had the appearance of a stalemate, Northern and Southern leaders knew better. Each victory weakened the Confederate army, while defeats still left the Union forces stronger than their opponents. The South remained in danger as long as Federal determination and pressure continued.

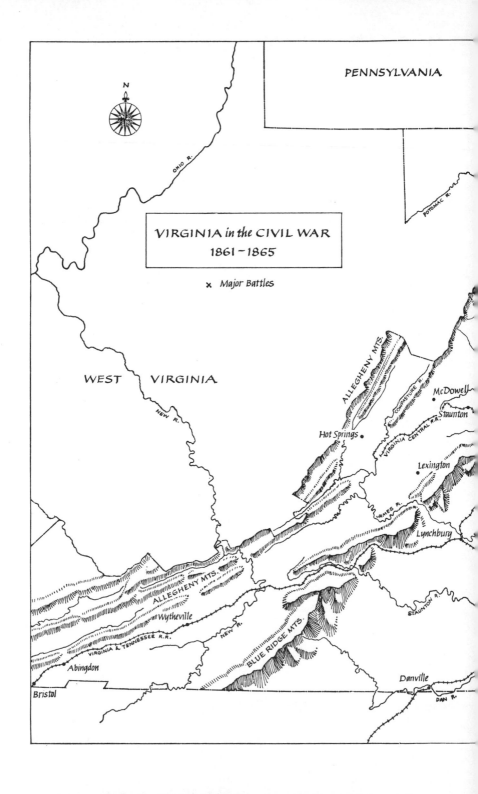

PENNSYLVANIA

OHIO R.

POTOMAC R.

VIRGINIA in the CIVIL WAR
1861 – 1865

✕ Major Battles

WEST VIRGINIA

NEW R.

ALLEGHENY MTS.

COWPASTURE R.

McDowell

Staunton

VIRGINIA CENTRAL R.R.

Hot Springs

Lexington

JAMES R.

Lynchburg

ALLEGHENY MTS.

Wytheville

STAUNTON R.

NEW R.

BLUE RIDGE MTS.

VIRGINIA & TENNESSEE R.R.

Abingdon

Bristol

Danville

DAN R.

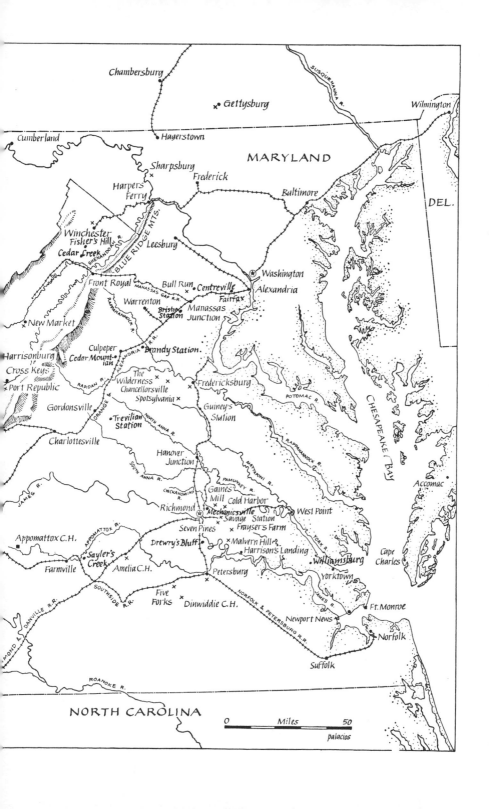

Chambersburg

Gettysburg

Wilmington

Cumberland

Hagerstown

MARYLAND

DEL.

Sharpsburg

Frederick

Harpers
Ferry

Baltimore

Winchester
Fisher's Hill
Cedar Creek

Leesburg

BLUE RIDGE MTS.

SHENANDOAH R.

Front Royal

Bull Run
Centreville

Washington
Alexandria

MANASSAS GAP R.R.

Fairfax

Warrenton

RAPPAHANNOCK R.

Bristoe
Station

Manassas
Junction

New Market

Culpeper
Cedar Mountian

Brandy Station.

Harrisonburg
Cross Keys

RAPIDAN R.

ORANGE & ALEXANDRIA R.R.

The
Wilderness
Chancellorsville
Spotsylvania

Fredericksburg

POTOMAC R.

CHESAPEAKE BAY

Port Republic

Gordonsville

Trevilian
Station

NORTH ANNA R.

Guiney's
Station

RAPPAHANNOCK R.

Charlottesville

SOUTH ANNA R.

Hanover
Junction

MATTAPONI R.

Accomac

JAMES R.

CHICKAHOMINY R.

PAMUNKEY R.

Gaines
Mill

Cold Harbor

Richmond

Mechanicsville

Savage Station

West Point

Appomattox C.H.

APPOMATTOX R.

Seven Pines

Frayser's Farm

YORK R.

Drewry's Bluff

Malvern Hill

Harrison's Landing

Williamsburg

Cape
Charles

Sayler's
Creek

Farmville

Amelia C.H.

Petersburg

Yorktown

RICHMOND & DANVILLE R.R.

SOUTHSIDE R.R.

Five
Forks

Dinwiddie C.H.

NORFOLK & PETERSBURG R.R.

JAMES R.

Ft. Monroe

Newport News

Norfolk

Suffolk

ROANOKE R.

NORTH CAROLINA

0   Miles   50

palacios

. VII .

Suffering Soldiers

As the major battleground for the Civil War in the East, Virginia also acquired two other dubious claims of distinction: it contained the largest number of military hospitals as well as the greatest concentration of prisoner-of-war compounds.

The happy shouting, band music, parades, and wild rush to enlistments at the start of the war caused people North and South to overlook the fact that many of the soldiers sent forward to battle would return as casualties. In the months that followed, once-gay city streets in Virginia became cluttered with injured men. They lay on blankets or stumbled about a town in search of help. Unprepared citizens rushed to give what assistance they could.

At first, enthusiasm to help prevailed over experience in helping. When a young Richmond girl bent over a wounded soldier and asked if he would like to have his face washed, the Confederate patiently replied: "Well, ma'am, it's been washed twenty times already but go ahead if you want to."

Care for the thousands upon thousands of ill soldiers was, like so many other measures in the hard-pressed Confederacy, belated and inadequate. The result was an appalling amount of suffering and an unbelievable loss of life. Surgeon Joseph Jones estimated after the war that every Johnny Reb was sick or wounded an average of six times; of the estimated 258,000 Southern soldiers who perished in the conflict, two-thirds of them died from illness and disease.

The C.S. Medical Department bore the responsibility of treating incapacitated servicemen. That agency had fewer than 3,000 physicians (of whom 755 were Virginians). Surgeon General Samuel Preston Moore, a highly capable administrator and strict disciplinarian, struggled heroically in accomplishing what he did. Yet Moore from the beginning faced the impossible task of trying to minister to a constant flood of sick and wounded with a system which was primitive, ill-organized, and lacking in every basic need.

Since perhaps as much as 90 percent of today's medical knowledge was unknown at the time of the Civil War, a seriously wounded or desperately ill soldier had little chance of recovery. Surgeons were few and terribly overworked. The Union blockade and lack of manufacturing facilities in the South made any medicine more precious than gold. Antebellum hospitals were not numerous because a "hospital" then was generally a repulsive medical storehouse where the unwanted were sent to die.

Conditions in the first makeshift military hospitals were horrifying. Many a soldier who survived the ordeal of battle perished slowly from improper treatment in germ-ridden medical centers. Epidemic diseases such as typhoid fever, measles, malaria, and intestinal disorders raged oftentimes out of control. Diarrhea and dysentery, rather than the enemy, were the biggest killers of the Civil War. By the late spring of 1862 a Confederate surgeon reported that the sick in Richmond were "dying by the thousands." Local gravediggers buried the dead en masse, and often in graves so shallow that the next rainstorm left their bodies exposed.

One of the field hospitals, established a mile or so behind the lines, that provided the first treatment of wounded soldiers. *Harper's Pictorial History of the Great Rebellion*

Every Virginia city alongside a railroad had at least one military hospital. The use of railroads to evacuate large numbers of wounded soldiers to treatment points safely behind battle zones was a milestone in Civil War medicine. Danville, Staunton, Bedford, Farmville, Petersburg, and Gordonsville maintained Confederate hospitals. The Charlottesville General Hospital, which received 1,200 wounded men after First Manassas, treated over 22,700 cases in the four years of war. Thirty-two buildings in Lynchburg—more then half of them former tobacco warehouses—became havens for sick soldiers. Some 10,000 patients received treatment there over a three-year period.

Richmond in 1861 contained three hospitals. As a transportation center, seat of government, and target of four years of fighting, it was the place to which most sick and wounded Johnny Rebs went. Richmond in time assumed the aura of a vast military hospital complex, with city residents as the staff. Some 60 percent of all Confederate wounded passed through the medical facilities of the capital.

Thirty-two general hospitals were constructed in Richmond for the care of Southern troops. Thirty or more businesses and private homes also became long-term official depositories for the crippled and weak. The largest of Richmond's medical centers was Winder Hospital on the city's western edge. Its ninety-eight pine buildings stood on an open expanse and could accommodate 4,300 patients at a time. A filthy trench surrounding the 125-acre compound became the dump for the hospital's refuse. For at least nine months of each year, the odor from Winder was unbearable to all but the most resolute soldiers and staff members.

Foremost among the private institutions was the

Sally Tompkins (1833–1916), a
demure spinster who operated one
of Richmond's most successful
military hospitals. Eleanor S.
Brockenbrough Library, The
Museum of the Confederacy

Judge Robertson home in the center of Richmond.
There twenty-seven-year-old Sally Tompkins opened a
small hospital in 1862 at her own expense. Through a
combination of attention, hard work, and assistance
from women volunteers, Tompkins maintained the
twenty-two-bed hospital with an incredible efficiency.
Of 1,333 wounded men sent there, only 73 died. When
the Confederate government ordered the private hospitals closed later in the war, a grateful President Davis
commissioned Tompkins a captain of cavalry so that her
hospital would remain open.

A wounded soldier looks at sprawling Chimborazo Hospital, in a rare photograph. The Museum of the Confederacy, courtesy of the Library of Congress

The most famous of Civil War medical centers was Chimborazo General Hospital. Located on Church Hill overlooking downtown Richmond and the James River, it had a breezy elevation plus a number of natural springs. Slaves constructed most of Chimborazo's 150 white one-story wards. Normal capacity was 3,000 patients. The staff consisted of fifty surgeons and a like number of volunteer matrons.

Dr. James B. McCaw, a New York University graduate in his late thirties, became surgeon-in-chief of the

new hospital. This "miracle man" operated Chimborazo without any government appropriation. The hospital produced its own soap, baked 10,000 loaves of bread
per day, maintained herds of cattle on neighboring farm-
land, had its own dairy, built five icehouses, and even
operated a canal boat to swap soldiers' clothing allow-
ances for vegetables, eggs, fruit, and other needed
goods. Wide, always clean streets separated the buildings; waste drained naturally into man-made gullies.

McCaw was a step beyond his contemporaries in

medical treatment. He utilized sunlight and fresh air as much as home remedies and herbal "medicines." Everything foul associated with hospitals in the past was removed. Convalescents regained their strength and assisted the staff by performing numerous chores. Chimborazo Hospital treated over 77,800 soldiers. Not until World War II did another military hospital match its low mortality rate. Most amazingly of all, the hospital was operating at a profit when the Confederacy ended.

Of course, Chimborazo was an exception to the rule. The avalanche of wounded Confederates—10,000 new cases poured into Richmond in the week following the 1864 Wilderness campaign—taxed the city's capacities to the fullest. Yet Richmond at the same time had to contend with another, even more undesirable torrent: captured Federal soldiers. Again the Confederacy, and in this case the Union as well, applied shortsighted and patchwork solutions to a problem of far-reaching and major dimensions.

Until 1861 prisoners of war had never been a major factor in America's wars. The few hundred enemy soldiers seized in previous conflicts took on-the-spot paroles with a simple promise not to bear arms again. When prisoner exchange was necessary, it was done on a one-to-one basis or along mathematical lines such as a captain for two lieutenants.

The Civil War changed all of that. Armies of enormous numbers grappling in combat produced captured soldiers in a volume never before encountered. The old system of paroles and exchanges no longer worked. North and South alike created military prison agencies almost as an afterthought, then left them to function largely on momentum. One authority has described the Confederate policy for prisoners of war as "the result of a series of accidents. . . . Prisons came into existence, without definite plans, to meet the exigencies of the moment." That is no exaggeration. A Southern chaplain remarked after the war: "There was not a Confederate official in the land who had any experience in taking care of prisoners of war."

Housing Federal prisoners became the duty of Richmond's provost marshal, John H. Winder. This abrasive officer had been a West Point professor when Jefferson Davis was a student at the academy. Winder was too old for field service in the 1860s; yet Davis liked him, gave Winder a brigadier general's commission, and assigned him the additional provost duty of watching over enemy prisoners.

Winder was totally ill-fitted for the job. He combined the belligerence of a military policeman with the sterner qualities of a martinet. One of his own men characterized the provost marshal as having a harsh face, cruel eyes, and a "mouth on which a smile seemed mockery." Winder became one of the most detested figures on either side during the war.

Late in July 1861 an initial batch of 775 Federal prisoners reached Richmond from the Manassas battlefield. Winder locked them in the Main Street railroad depot. As more captured soldiers arrived in ensuing months, the provost marshal commandeered factories and warehouses and converted them into temporary prisons by barring the windows and installing more secure entrances.

Ligon's Warehouse and Tobacco Factory, for example, became a brief home for 600 Federal soldiers. Once or twice a month, some 150–250 prisoners left Richmond for compounds farther south (such as Salisbury, N.C.). Richmond's prison population by year's end was down

to 1,000 men, the lowest number the capital had for the remainder of the war. Officials began cleaning and whitewashing the old warehouse prisons for conversion into military hospitals. Then the volume of prisoners began to increase and continued to climb throughout the war because all Federals captured in Virginia went to Richmond first before reassignment to a prison elsewhere in the South.

Virginia's most notorious soldier-prison (but by no means its worst) was the former warehouse of Libby and Son, Ship Chandlers and Grocers. The structure was actually three connecting warehouses, three stories high in front and four stories in the rear as the land sloped down to nearby James River. Libby Prison opened in March 1862 as a receiving station for all "fresh" prisoners. Ultimately it became an officer's compound. Libby's population was generally about 1,300 men who had nothing to do but police their cramped quarters and endure poor rations, every breed of vermin, and unsympathetic guards.

The major prison in Richmond for Federal enlisted men was Belle Isle. The normally beautiful island in the James just above the downtown area sloped on all sides to the water's edge. A low hill near the center was ideal for guard posts, and the rapid flow of the river at that point made escape extremely dangerous. In time, as many as 8,000 Federals were jammed together on Belle Isle. The ground was constantly wet; a few tents were the only shelters provided; food, clothing, and medicine were always in critically short supply. Wintertime brought indescribable suffering. More than one despondent Billy Yank accepted death in the river to life on the island.

Six other prisons existed in wartime Richmond. In each, Federal soldiers found themselves rooming with Confederate deserters, political prisoners, murderers, and thieves. Castle Godwin fortunately had a short existence. In prewar days the small building was McDaniel's Negro Jail, with its name giving a clear idea of the nature of its facilities. A successor to Castle Godwin was the larger and more notorious Castle Thunder. This former tobacco warehouse housed every kind of offender during the war years, with little segregation made between a soldier and a sociopath. Provost marshal authorities called the prison Castle Thunder, a Richmond newspaper explained, because it was meant to be "indicative of Olympian vengeance upon offenders against her laws."

Federal prisoners in Richmond soon comprised a

Belle Isle, in the James River just above downtown Richmond.
Harper's Weekly

third of the capital's population. The city hardly needed those residents. Contending armies were feeding off the state; Richmond's numbers had already swollen beyond control with Confederate government workers and officials, wounded men from both sides, transient soldiers, and refugees. More prisoners also meant more prison-guard units, which in turn meant more mouths to feed. Virginians were as reluctant to keep the prisoners as they were to be there.

Both North and South were so burdened with prisoners of war by the summer of 1862 that the two governments initiated an official cartel for releasing captured soldiers. The exchange worked only for a few months. The whole system rested on gentlemen's agreements; and once the Civil War passed the boundaries of gentlemanly conduct, prisoner exchange disintegrated. In 1863 Northern authorities announced an end to the cartel. Prisoners of war would be held indefinitely thereafter.

By the autumn of that year, 15,000 emaciated and/or sick Federals packed Richmond's prisons. Lack of basic necessities was a common characteristic of each military jail. Rare indeed was the prison where malnutrition, scurvy, exposure, filth, and chronic diarrhea were not cellmates. Neglect and cruel treatment became a way of life for captured soldiers.

It was impossible for the beleaguered and strapped Confederacy to provide adequate care. The North could have done so with its imprisoned Confederates but did not. Rumors of the treatment of Federal prisoners of war seeped northward. Officials in Washington, accepting as truth even the most exaggerated of stories, released them to the public and branded them diabolical acts perpetrated by Confederate authorities. Retaliatory actions followed. Southern prisoners of war soon encountered reduced rations and clothing, limits on firewood, and less medical attention. The real suffering at Libby and Belle Isle had horrible parallels in what captured Southerners endured at such Federal prisons as Point Lookout, Fort Delaware, and Elmira.

As Grant moved on Richmond in the spring of 1864, Winder ordered most of the capital's prison population transferred farther south. Six tobacco warehouses in Danville became the state's principal depository for Federal soldiers in the last year of the war. However, the largest contingent of Union prisoners went to a hastily and halfheartedly constructed prison-camp in southern Georgia. It was officially called Camp Sumter. History knows it as Andersonville. Over 13,000 of the Civil War's 56,000 prison deaths occurred there.

The fires of controversy that erupted during the Civil War over treatment of prisoners of war smolder on. A few buildings used as military hospitals still stand in Richmond, Lynchburg, Gordonsville, Danville, and elsewhere. Such structures, as well as the prison locations, are reminders that for every man killed in action, two soldiers died behind the lines from sickness. Those sites also stand as monuments, not to soldiers gallantly killed in battle but to sick men who underwent the agony of death slowly and silently amid hundreds of suffering companions.

They may have been the greatest heroes of them all.

. VIII .

The Homefront

Contrary to embellished novels and Hollywood productions, the Southern Confederacy was not an idyllic land of magnolias and mint juleps, or of sweet springtimes and gay spirits, or of unity and fraternity. Such were the 1861 dreams of its people. Reality came with harshness and pain. Want replaced wishes.

State and national leaders offered few solutions to social problems because the Confederacy and its component parts dwelled most often in a political vacuum. President Davis quickly learned that a government based on state rights could not wage a concerted war effectively. Yet his every effort at nationalization met strong opposition. On the other hand, the Confederate Congress was so unwilling to exert legislative leadership that General Lee once accused the congressmen of being unable "to do anything except eat peanuts and chew tobacco."

Virginia's John Letcher was the governor with whom Davis enjoyed the closest confidence and cooperation. However, Letcher's wartime problems were equally severe. He and the state legislature were always aware of Virginia's illnesses but always unsure of the long-range remedies. Letcher had no bloc of supporters inside the General Assembly, and he and state legislators had a mutual distrust of one another. The governor once referred to the "criminal indifference" of the assembly with regard to the needs of the oppressed state. The legislature reacted sharply to what it viewed as Letcher's overuse of executive power. The continual friction left Virginia citizens to fend for themselves most of the time.

As the war continued, Southern governments demanded more and more sacrifices while resources declined and prices soared. Normal life ceased. Changes wrought by the long struggle were sometimes violent, sometimes subtle, and almost always cancerous. No Virginia community or citizen completely escaped the plague of war. Many were destroyed by it, others came to terms with it, and a few even profited from it.

Richmond was illustrative of the Confederacy's two faces: luxury and poverty. The luxury was enjoyed by those who had either abundant means or else connections with blockade-running and black-marketeering. They brought a flavor of romance to the last stand of Southern civilization. Not only did the well-to-do entertain regularly and relish occasional bountiful meals; they also colored the Confederacy by their appearance. One young socialite who wrote glowingly of attending the funeral of "a spotless knight" at well-kept Hollywood Cemetery seemed unaware that Oakwood Cemetery on the other side of Richmond was rapidly expanding with the unknown dead of battles and disease.

Down below the elite level, among the great masses of plain folk, was poverty. Social disruption during the war, especially that caused by the Federal armies, struck the hardest in Virginia. Yet the Old Dominion was not alone in the new nation. From the outset, the Confederacy faced serious and rarely addressed shortages.

President Davis preferred the role of commander in chief to inspirational leader. The Confederate Congress seemed more disposed toward personal arguments than

In their crowded single room, a mother and daughter scrape corn from cobs preparatory to making bread. *Harper's Weekly*

to public needs. Numerous critics branded it "a college debating society," while a Virginian in the War Department observed: "Certainly no deliberative body ever met in this state with less of statesmanship in it."

Governors throughout the South refused to cooperate for the national good. Transportational facilities dete-

riorated. Hoarding and speculation became rampant. Medicines, not permitted to pass through the Federal naval blockade, were in short supply for the armies and practically nonexistent for the civilian population. Food, clothing, cloth, soap, paper, and metal products of any kind became increasingly scarce. While Richmond's affluent class appeared to enjoy a life of continuity with but minor inconveniences, most of the capital's residents were reduced in time to living in basements or single rooms and waging a constant battle against starvation.

Tribulations in Richmond provide the clearest picture of need and suffering, but it should be remembered that acute want was present throughout the state. As early as April 1862, Mrs. Margaret Preston of Lexington wrote in her journal: "How I loathe the word *war*! Our schools are closed, stores shut up, goods not to be bought, or so exorbitant we must do without. I actually dressed my baby all winter in calico dresses made out of the lining of an old dressing gown."

Four months later Lucy Johnston Ambler observed from her Fauquier County home: "Everything looks very gloomy. From having a comfortable table, I am reduced to a bacon bone. The Yankeys have overrun my garden and injured what they did not take away. . . . I have a very sick grandchild and several servants sick with no suitable medicine. May God give me grace and strength to bear my burden knowing that."

A Confederate surgeon passed through Culpeper in the autumn of 1863 and informed his wife: "The part of Virginia through which we have marched has been totally devastated. It is now nothing but one vast track of desolation, without a fence or a planted field of any kind. I do not understand how the people exist."

Federal destruction took a severe toll, to be sure, but internal collapses played an equally deadly part as well in the short life of the Confederacy. A survey of inflation inside the wartime South gives a picture of economic chaos traditonally masked by the valor of the gray-clad armies in the field.

In late spring 1861 the Confederate government began issuing $20 million in three-year paper notes. By August of that year, over $100 million worth of notes were in circulation, these treasury bills payable "six months after the ratification of peace between the Confederate States of America and the United States." This unsupported currency was but the starting point. Soon the entire South was half-buried under a cascade of paper money issued by states, cities, businesses, banks, and anyone else with an engraver and a printing press.

The results were predictable. By late 1862 available money bought only a third of what it could have purchased twelve months earlier. The price of potatoes had doubled, flour had tripled, meat had quadrupled. Sugar was ten times what it had been; coffee prices were literally out of sight.

In 1863 a Confederate private earned $11 per month. A barrel of flour was then $300, a bushel of cornmeal was $80, a turkey cost $60, and a pound of butter brought at least $15 when available. As Christmas 1864 approached, a Richmond woman stated: "Day by day our wants and privations increase . . . in the cheerless season to which we look forward with dread."

Houses by then were cold because firewood did not exist or was too exorbitant to be affordable. Just boarding a horse in Richmond cost $300 a month. Flour was $500 per barrel. A Confederate dollar was worth so little that it took fifty-three of them to get a gold dollar. A Richmond shopper once moaned: "I took my money in the market-basket and brought home the purchases in my pocketbook."

A month before war's end, bacon was $20 per pound, flour $1,200 a barrel, butter a minimum of $25 a pound. Although the Confederate soldier then made

$18 monthly, his money was of scant value. A government worker noted in March 1865: "Richmond is rapidly approaching a state of famine." Occupation by Federal troops the next month was almost a blessing.

Exactly what inflation and its associated evils wrought was clearly evident by the mid-year of the Civil War. In January 1863 Confederate war clerk J. B. Jones noted of life in Richmond: "A portion of the people look like vagabonds. We see men and women and children in the streets in dingy and delapidated clothes; and some seem gaunt and pale with hunger—the speculators, and thieving quartermasters and commissaries only, looking sleek and comfortable."

Jones understated the true situation. Impoverished mothers and wives unraveled old stockings to remove the worn threads before reknitting them. "New" jackets were patchwork affairs made from tattered overcoats. Window curtains became petticoats; draperies soon appeared as dresses.

Even sending a letter to a soldier required great effort. Paper came from old ledgers, family albums, books, even wallpaper. Pokeberry or persimmon juice, with a rusty nail used to darken the color, produced a passable ink. Glue for sealing a letter could be made by mixing peach gum with cornstarch.

Tree leaves and pine needles repacked mattresses. Peanut oil mixed with lard served as lantern fuel. Indeed, peanuts came into full play as imitations of chocolate and coffee. Rye, corn, chestnuts, sweet potatoes, and other commodities became coffee substitutes, with sorghum a popular replacement for sugar.

Hunger occupied the thoughts of most people because it was so widespread. A black joke in Richmond was that rats came out in the kitchens to beg for food, while half-starved cats staggered around the houses because the rats were too emaciated to be edible.

One group of women saw no humor in their plight. Early on the morning of April 2, 1863, a large number of them (with some young boys also in attendance) gathered at Capitol Square to complain about lack of food. Their numbers soon increased to about 1,000 people. The mob then marched downhill to the businesses along Main Street.

As frightened shopkeepers tried to close their doors, the press of the crowd broke them open. Arms and aprons were soon full of food, but a chain reaction to the "Bread Riot" now occurred. Rowdier elements began smashing doors and windows of all shops. Looters were walking away with everything from washtubs and ladies' slippers to clothespins and hats.

Mayor Joseph Mayo and Governor Letcher rushed to the scene, along with the City Battalion of troops. The mayor threatened to have the soldiers open fire if this public disturbance did not cease. Jefferson Davis soon arrived after being drawn by the noise. The president stood in his carriage and made a noble appeal. He warned the swarming crowd that such lawlessness would keep other food from the city. Moreover, Davis added, the muskets leveled at the women would be far better used pointing at Yankees.

The women slowly dispersed. Some thirty ringleaders were arrested but soon released. Yet the situation did not improve. A few months later, a teenaged girl stated: "In Richmond we have never known such a scarcity of food—such absolute want of the necessities of life."

Pressures of civil war likewise brought a breakdown of morality in many other areas of Virginia. Even in the remote southwestern region of the state, bands of guer-

A Northern artist's conception of the "Bread Riot" in Richmond.
Frank Leslie's Illustrated Newspaper, courtesy of the Eleanor S.
Brockenbrough Library, The Museum of the Confederacy

rillas and bushwhackers practiced lawlessness with unceasing cruelty. Roadside robberies became commonplace in city and country. So did public drunkenness. The large number of speculators and black-marketeers led one newspaper to state bluntly: "Every man in this community is swindling everybody else."

Richmond again serves as a horrible example of the decay that undermined Virginia. A newspaper early in the war bemoaned the fact that the capital was "full of the vilest licentiousness. Among all loathsome vices imported, gambling [is] so prominent and brazen as to defy public decency as well as law." Pandemonium seemed the order of the day, another editor asserted. Thieves and robbers prowled every dark street; assaults had become ordinary events; arrests for intoxication and prostitution were daily occurrences.

By 1863 Richmond had swollen to 128,000 residents—almost four times its prewar size. The city was virtually overrun by transients, soldiers, refugees, spies, prostitutes, and adventurers. One section of the capital had forty gambling houses that sold smuggled goods to the highest bidder. Governor Letcher decried the situation in a message to the General Assembly. "A reckless spirit of money making seems to have taken possession of the public mind," Letcher stated. "Avarice has become a ruling passion . . . patriotism is second to 'love of money.'"

Lawlessness reached its crowning indignity on November 18 of that year, when thieves burglarized the home of Provost Marshal Gen. John Winder.

Another problem that never became a crisis was Virginia's slave population. About 490,000 blacks were in the state at the time of secession. The threat of a slave insurrection amid the confusion of war was a strong possibility. No such mass uprising took place, even though an occasional plot materialized. Thus could Margaret Preston of Lexington write in the spring of 1862: "One thing surprises me—the entire quietness and subordination of negroes. We have slept all winter with the doors of our house unlocked. . . . Some thousands of dollars worth of silver is in the dining room, unguarded. Would I get my Northern friends to believe that?"

During the war some blacks volunteered, and larger numbers were impressed, to perform many tasks for the Confederate war effort. They constructed earthworks, labored in ordnance, quartermaster, and commissary departments, served as blacksmiths, cooks, shoemakers, and coal miners. Others drove army wagons, manned riverboats, and helped keep the railroads operating. Those blacks who remained at homeplaces showed remarkable fidelity. One of their number, Booker T. Washington, had an explanation: "To defend and protect the women and children who were left on the plantation when the white males went to war, the slaves would have laid down their lives."

Many doubtless would have done so. On the other hand, thousands of slaves took advantage of the presence of Union troops along the Virginia coast to run away to freedom. A Federal official reported "an almost stampede of slaves" taking place when Union forces massed in 1862 at Norfolk and along the coast. At least 5,700 former Virginia slaves joined the Federal armies. They increased the strength of the Northern forces while decreasing to an even greater extent the state's already-strapped agricultural production.

In the face of hardships at every turn, Virginia womenfolk displayed amazing determination and resilience.

They supported the war as much as their soldiers, for defense of home and liberties were as dear to them. The term "Yankees" assumed all the vile overtones that "Redcoats" had carried in the American Revolution. Many women, especially the younger ones, underwent a marked change of attitude toward outsiders from pre-war hospitality to wartime hostility.

Untold numbers of women sewed uniforms and knitted socks for relatives and friends in service. As the war progressed, their labors went in other directions: scraping old linen into piles of soft lint and cutting strips from cotton garments for use as bandages in the hospitals.

Women workers in a bullet-making armory. *Harper's Pictorial History of the Great Rebellion*

Hundreds of women broke social barriers by taking jobs in government agencies as munition workers and clerks. Others volunteered as nurses in foul-smelling and disease-ridden hospitals. So many women sought to pick up the educational slack that the word "schoolmistress" came in time to replace "schoolmaster." Almost every Virginia family seemed to lose a husband, father, son, or brother in the fighting, but the women absorbed their grief and silently continued to do what they could for their country.

It was never easy. In addition to all the social and economic ills, women in many locales had to combat the ravages of epidemics such as smallpox, scarlet fever, and pneumonia. Some watched alone as children slowly died from lack of medicines. More than one mother was forced to prepare the body and dig the grave for a son or daughter.

In February 1865 Fauquier County's Amanda Klipstein embodied the spirit of her class when she wrote her husband-soldier: "My dear you know, or ought to know . . . how lonely we all feel without you. . . . Now my dear don't you think hard of it. It has been so cold [here] that it has been nothing else much done but try to keep warm."

. IX .

Joy and Gloom in 1863

Cavalry raids made the headlines as the Civil War
entered its second year—a year in which Lee would
see his most brilliant victory and his most stunning defeat.

John S. Mosby hardly looked the part of a dashing
horseman, nor was he trained in warfare. He was a
small, thin man, a lawyer by profession and well-versed
in both Latin and Greek. Yet darting eyes that missed
little, quick thinking, plus an indefinable intuition,
stamped Mosby as a natural leader of cavalrymen. He
became colonel of an 800-man battalion of "Partisan
Rangers." However, Mosby preferred to stage a strike
with no more than seventy-five riders at a time. He and
his band established an early reputation for being invincible by night and invisible by day.

Under cover of darkness on March 8, 1863, "The
Gray Ghost" and twenty-nine of his men raided Fairfax
Court House miles behind enemy lines. Mosby personally roused Gen. E. H. Stoughton from bed and made
him a prisoner of war. The Confederates also seized
thirty-two other Federals, fifty-eight horses, and much
badly needed equipment before making their escape.
What made this feat all the more embarrassing for the
Federals was the fact that Stoughton at the time was
searching for Mosby's whereabouts.

The subsequent hit-and-run exploits of Mosby kept
Union forces in northern Virginia off-balance. In the last

half of the war, the area west of Alexandria and east of
Winchester was known as "Mosby's Confederacy." Federal troops combed woods and backcountry in repeated
attempts to bag the raider. As they did so, the partisan
rangers continued their unpredictable and dramatic for-
ays. One of Mosby's most outstanding feats came in
1864, when his men captured a train near Harpers Ferry
and carried off its cargo of some $173,000 in Federal
greenbacks.

Barely a week after Mosby's escapade at Fairfax,

Colonel John S. Mosby (1833–1916), hatless and clean-shaven, standing in the middle of some of his Partisan Rangers. The Museum of the Confederacy, courtesy of the Maryland Historical Society, Baltimore

Union cavalry under Gen. William Averell started across the Rappahannock River to operate in the Culpeper area. Confederate horsemen under Gen. Fitzhugh Lee (the army commander's nephew) intercepted the Federals at Kelly's Ford. Averell withdrew after brisk fighting. Confederate losses, twice those of their opponents, marked an important transition in cavalry operations.

Until that time, Southern horsemen had been decidedly superior in every respect to their Northern counterparts. Federal cavalry, on the other hand, had gained in

The Federal cavalry fights with renewed vigor at Kelly's Ford. *The Soldier in Our Civil War*

both numbers and experience as the war continued. They had fought so long in north-central Virginia that they knew the land almost as well as the inhabitants. Along with confidence, Union mounted brigades had also acquired new leaders who were a notch above their predecessors in ability. Kelly's Ford marked the beginning of equality between Northern and Southern cavalry.

Meanwhile, two mighty armies still watched each other from opposite sides of the Rappahannock. Neither host had moved from winter quarters established after the Fredericksburg campaign, but important changes had taken place in each army. Lee's forces had deteriorated badly during the cold months of inactivity. Horses had starved to death while soldiers grubbed for wild onions and sassafras roots. Pneumonia, scurvy, and always present diarrhea had taken a deadly toll.

The South's limited manpower all but dictated that the Confederacy concentrate its troops for a better chance at success. This basic premise ran counter to the Davis administration's insistence that every threatened area be protected. In April the War Department pulled Longstreet with two of his divisions from Lee's army and sent them toward Suffolk to confront Federals moving inland from the Virginia and North Carolina coasts. This depletion left Lee with 60,000 impoverished troops on the main line.

An opposite development had occurred with the Army of the Potomac. It greatly increased in strength that spring under a new commander. General Joseph Hooker was ambitious, unpopular among his fellow officers, and a man of questionable morals. Charles Francis Adams considered him "little better than a West Point adventurer," and he added that Hooker's head-

General Joseph Hooker (1815–1879). *Harper's Pictorial History of the Great Rebellion*

quarters was "a combination of barroom and brothel."

Two things can be said to Hooker's credit. Like McClellan, he was a superb organizer. He spent the winter of 1863 building his army to 130,000 men and instilling high morale inside the ranks. Second, Hooker devised an offensive plan for destroying Lee's army that almost succeeded. Almost.

Hooker's strategy called for three simultaneous operations. Federal cavalry would gallop around Lee and toward Richmond to disrupt army communications and create confusion behind enemy lines. General John Sedgwick and two Federal corps would push against Fredericksburg to occupy Lee's attention. Hooker with three other corps would secretly march west, cross the Rappahannock and Rapidan rivers, move south through the densely wooded Wilderness area, and assail both the flank and rear of the Confederate army. Two remaining Federal corps would be held in reserve to move where needed.

Lee would thus be caught between the arms of a giant vise. He would have to come out of his impregnable defenses and fight. If Lee attempted instead to retreat, his army would pass in front of Hooker's 70,000 men. That wing by itself outnumbered Lee's army and would surely emerge the victor in an open battle.

On April 27 the Federal offensive began. Hooker's forces covered forty miles in three days; and by the thirtieth, they were at Chancellorsville. This was not a village but an important crossroads deep in the Wilderness. An excited Hooker chortled: "I have Lee in one hand and Richmond in the other." Hooker had something else too: military blindness. The eyes of his army—his cavalry—were off on a diversionary raid and could provide no information as to Lee's movements.

Simply because the odds against him were so great, Lee had nothing to lose by taking enormous risks. One of the Confederate general's assets was rarely doing what his opponent expected. He displayed that trait in the spring of 1863 with a boldness that resulted in what has been called "Lee's perfect victory."

Lee dismissed the Federal cavalry raid as little more than a nuisance, which it turned out to be. General George Stoneman and his 15,000 horsemen sent Richmond into a brief state of frenzy but broke off their raid ten miles from the capital and its thin line of defenders. Lee's cavalry served him much better, for Stuart discovered Hooker's main movement to the west.

Now it was Lee's turn to act. The major Federal thrust would be from the area of Chancellorsville. Lee left 10,000 troops under Gen. Jubal Early to confront Sedgwick's 47,000 Federals at Fredericksburg, then speedily shifted the rest of his army toward the Wilderness. Hooker's lead elements were just emerging into open and maneuverable country when they bumped into the van of Lee's forces.

The bombacity and confidence in Hooker abruptly disappeared. Over the protests of his generals, he ordered the Federal troops back into the Wilderness and hastily began constructing earthworks. The Union commander who had earlier stated that the secret to success was "fight, fight, fight" had inexplicably surrendered the initiative to Lee.

On the night of May 1, Lee and Jackson sat on cracker boxes at a wooded crossroads. There Lee made the most daring decision of his career. Jackson's corps of 28,000 would again make a forced march around the enemy's western flank, which, anchored on no natural obstacle, was "dangling in the air." Once Jackson had marched across Hooker's front and was in position, he would attack and drive the enemy units into one another. Lee, with only 14,000 soldiers, would stand between Hooker's 70,000 men and Richmond while the flank movement was underway. Confederates would then launch assaults from two different directions.

It took Jackson most of May 2 to cover the twelve miles on snaking country roads that ran south, west, and north. Shortly after 5 P.M., his troops were facing east and poised along either side of the Orange Turnpike. Jackson calmly gave the signal. Screams of the "Rebel Yell" broke the silence as Southerners rushed forward in a line two miles wide.

Federal soldiers on that flank had stacked arms and were cooking their evening meal when Jackson's men struck. Hooker's right wing collapsed. In minutes, a full Union corps was a mass of frantic men in headlong flight. Soldiers and horses, cannon, wagons, and ambulances all dashed through the woods toward safety. A

Lee and Jackson in the Wilderness as they planned the flank attack on Hooker's exposed right at Chancellorsville. Sketch by Virginia artist William Sheppard. *Century War Book*

Massachusetts infantryman recalled that "along the road it was pandemonium; on the side of the road it was chaos."

Jackson's lines slashed for two miles through woods, undergrowth, and shattered Federal units. Darkness began to settle. The Confederate attack was losing momentum at the same time that Union officers were improvising new defensive positions.

Jackson was eager to continue pressing forward. After nightfall, and for the only time in the war, the Confederate Cromwell made a personal reconnaissance in his front. Confusion still reigned in the dark woods. As Jackson and his staff were riding back to their own lines, Confederates mistook them for Federal cavalry and opened fire. Several horsemen were killed, and Jackson reeled in the saddle from two bullet wounds.

The next day, with Stuart in temporary command of Jackson's corps, the Confederates resumed their assaults. They gained valuable ground, including an elevated ridge from which Southern artillery raked the Federal lines. A stunned Hooker was of no help as his invading army fought for survival against the now-reunited forces of Lee and Jackson.

At Fredericksburg, meanwhile, Sedgwick had broken through the Confederate defenses and was moving west along the turnpike toward Chancellorsville. Lee met this new threat promptly. He dispatched a division which collided with Sedgwick's force at Salem Church. A second Confederate division reached the field on May 4, just as Early's men were also approaching from Fredericksburg.

The Federals fought well and held firm for a time. Soon under attack from two different directions, Sedgwick abandoned the idea of joining Hooker and retired

across the Rappahannock. Lee retraced his steps to re-
new the offensive against Hooker. By then, the Union
general previously hailed as "Fighting Joe" had had
enough. He ordered the Army of the Potomac, a full
third of which had seen no action, back across the river.

Chancellorsville was a spectacular achievement for
the Confederates. It was a battle they supposedly could
not win, but did. However, overlooked by many in the
celebrations was the crippling cost of victory. Lee suffered 12,900 casualties, over a fifth of his command.
While Hooker's 17,300 losses were greater in number,
they were considerably less in proportion.

This engagement brought an aura of invincibility to
the Southern force defending Virginia. "There never
were such men in an army before," a proud Lee stated.
"They will go anywhere and do anything if properly
led." Nevertheless, the Army of the Potomac remained
intact and more powerful even in defeat.

Elation in the state over Chancellorsville vanished a
week later with the greatest personal loss the Confederacy suffered during the war. On May 10 Stonewall Jackson died of complications from his wounds. A nation
fell stricken with grief. The largest crowd in the annals
of the Confederacy filed past his bier in Richmond. A
British newspaperman spoke for the South when he
wrote: "One of the purest, most guileless, most unselfish
spirits ever lent to earth . . . has gone at a moment when
nothing can be added to his earthly fame."

When Jackson passed from the scene, so did the military miracles that Lee had woven the previous year. Se-
crecy, great flank movements, surprise—all were gone.
Lee alone was left in Virginia to keep the flame alive in
the war's second half, and the great army leader so outstanding in the old school of field commanders could

Jackson's attack at Chancellorsville. *Century War Book*

not win the kind of battles that the expanding Civil War was generating.

Lee deeply mourned the loss of "my right arm," as he termed Jackson. Yet he had to turn his thoughts to taking advantage of a foe knocked back on his heels at Chancellorsville. The decision by Lee to invade the North again was based on many of the factors that had prompted Lee's advance into Maryland a year earlier— with one exception. The 1862 offensive rested on hope; the second one was a move more of desperation.

For a month after Chancellorsville, the Southern army filled its ranks and refitted itself as best it could. Lee's forces were massing around Culpeper for the new campaign when Federal cavalry on June 9 sought to strike a part of Lee's encampment. The raid initially caught Stuart and his troopers by surprise. Stuart rushed to meet the threat at Brandy Station. Soon 20,000 mounted soldiers, equally divided, were engaged in the largest cavalry battle ever fought on American soil.

Hour after hour occurred frantic charges against massed artillery, head-on collisions between galloping lines, hand-to-hand fighting, with sabers flashing and revolvers firing at close range. The battle raged across open fields, along country roads, and all around a prominence known as Fleetwood Hill. By midfternoon the Confederates held the field and claimed victory. Dead horses and 1,200 killed and wounded soldiers lay everywhere. One of the injured was Lee's son "Rooney," a huge brigadier general described as "too big for a man and not big enough to be a horse." Brandy Station was a clear signal that Union cavalry could now hold their own against Stuart's men. The engagement seriously tarnished the fame and pride of Stuart.

Lee put his whole army into motion a week later. At

first, all went well. Confederates trapped a Federal division at Winchester and seized 3,000 prisoners. Lee passed through Maryland and entered Pennsylvania. His army hardly looked like its exalted reputation. Fully half of the men were barefooted; shirts and trousers were mismatched as well as patchworked; hats were a luxury which few enjoyed; hunger was present throughout the ranks, but so was high morale.

The Army of the Potomac gave chase. By then it was under its last and best commander, Gen. George G. Meade. A dedicated soldier in his early forties, Meade was married to a Virginia girl who was the sister-in-law of former governor and now Confederate general Henry A. Wise. Meade was solid rather than brilliant. He assumed army command only three days before the largest battle so far in the war began.

General George G. Meade (1815–1872). *Harper's Weekly*

Logic rarely characterized the Confederate effort at Gettysburg. Stuart's cavalry led the way north. They conducted diversionary raids, kept Union horsemen occupied, and confiscated 125 army wagons loaded with supplies. In the process, however, they left Lee groping blindly on the advance and never quite sure where his adversary was. Once contact occurred with the enemy, the smaller Confederate army attacked from the west and north. Meade's superior numbers took positions along a range of hills and fought defensively for three bloody days.

Gettysburg's climax came on July 3, when Lee ordered an assault on the Union center. Spearheading the attack was Gen. George E. Pickett's all-Virginia division of 6,300 men. Forty percent of them were killed, wounded, or captured in the ill-fated charge against massed infantry and artillery. The 1st Virginia, a proud unit with roots extending back to the French and Indian War of colonial days, lost 120 of 160 men in the July 3 charge. Every officer was killed or wounded except one lieutenant—and he was captured. Lee's total casualties were 28,000, more than a third of the army's strength at the time. Victory cost the North 23,000 Federals.

The Army of Northern Virginia was never the same again. Its officer losses were so great as to dictate a complete restructuring of the chain-of-command system on division, brigade, and regimental levels. In a phrase, Lee at Gettysburg missed the bungling of Hooker and the brilliance of Jackson.

Both armies returned to Virginia. The military situation resumed its old pattern of Rebels and Yanks facing each other along the Rappahannock-Rapidan line. The Northern ranks were well-fed and well-equipped. Lee's army searched and scratched for every necessity of life.

Defeat at Gettysburg of a supposedly invincible army, plus the loss of Vicksburg and the Mississippi River at precisely the same time, cast a pall over the Confederacy. A Richmond girl commented: "Every countenance was overspread with gloom, and doubt took the place of hope."

As autumn came, Lee agreed to dispatch Longstreet and two divisions to the hard-pressed Confederate forces in Tennessee. Lee then got word that Meade had similarly transferred two full corps to the Western theater. The Confederate general went on the offensive to exploit this weakness. Lee's hope was to get Meade away from Culpeper, a strategic point which offered several avenues for Federal advance. The Confederates thereupon began a circuitous march around Meade's flank toward Washington.

Meade cautiously fell back in front of Lee. On October 14 A. P. Hill came upon what he thought was an isolated Federal force at Bristoe Station. Hill rashly ordered two brigades to attack. They quickly found themselves in a cross fire from two Federal corps. The Confederates suffered 1,500 losses in the brief and one-sided contest. Lee soon discovered that he could not continue his advance because of lack of supplies. Reluctantly, the Confederate army returned to the Rappahannock country and its rail connections with Richmond.

Washington was safe, so Meade edged back to his former position. On November 7 Federals fought their way across the Rappahannock at Kelly's Ford and Rappahannock Station. Lee retired to the south side of the Rapidan. Meade continued moving forward. Reports from Stuart convinced Lee that the Union army was seeking to pass Lee's front and march on Richmond. Lee ordered his forces to move out and prepare for battle.

For four days, November 26–30, Confederates dug earthworks along Mine Run. The intricate network of trenches reflected Lee's skill in field fortifications. Meade deployed his forces to attack; but cannon fire from the Southerners, the tangled, rough country where the Union army was massed, and bitterly cold weather—as well perhaps as memories of Lee's vicious assaults at Gettysburg—all persuaded Meade to abandon the campaign. The Federals reoccupied Culpeper, which became a Federal advance base in Virginia for the remainder of the war.

Once again, on opposite banks of a river, the two armies slowly settled into winter hibernation. Both sides had been battered and bloodied to new levels by the fighting of 1863, and more was to come. Thousands of Lee's soldiers found a measure of comfort that winter in the largest religious revival ever to sweep through an American army. Opposing pickets regularly exchanged conversation and swapped items such as coffee and tobacco. The strains of "Home, Sweet Home" that drifted skyward with the smoke from clusters of log cabins and lean-tos had a double meaning. One was a weariness with war; the other, a common bond between enemy troops simultaneously practicing fraternization and fratricide.

. X .

Wilderness to Petersburg

Winter was still winding down when the fighting of 1864 began. Confederate officials at the time were convinced that any threat on Richmond would come from the Army of the Potomac. Thus, with Lee holding Meade along the Rappahannock line, the Southern capital was virtually unguarded. Federals by then were also aware of Stuart's weakened cavalry arm. His mounted units had shrunk pitifully in size, and many of the horses had of necessity been transferred to the artillery during the months of inactivity. Stuart was still in the throes of rebuilding his command.

The opportunity seemed right to Northern authorities for a stab at Richmond. Union horsemen probably could not seize the city, but they might be able to free 15,000 prisoners of war there. Surely the Federal cavalry would send consternation rippling across Virginia and gain a psychological edge for the North before major campaigning resumed in the spring.

In late February the operation began. Some 3,000 mounted Federals rode from their encampments and proceeded south around Lee's army. At their head was Judson Kilpatrick, an ambitious, restless brigadier general in his mid-twenties. Commensurate with Kilpatrick's advance, 400 picked cavalry under one-legged Col. Ulric Dahlgren galloped west and turned back in a sweeping arc designed to bring them in on Richmond's exposed west side.

Kilpatrick and Dahlgren both left such a path of loot-

ing and burning in their wake that farmers for miles
around grabbed shotguns and gave pursuit as snipers. A
now-unnerved Kilpatrick turned his column toward
Williamsburg and the safety of Union lines. Dahlgren's
small band proceeded through snow and sleet to the
outskirts of the capital.

A well-aimed volley from variously armed young
boys, old men, factory workers, and the like sent Dahlgren's troopers scurrying away to join Kilpatrick. Pieces
of Confederate home-guard units gave chase. They
caught up with the Federals in King and Queen County,
killed Dahlgren, and scattered his force. Found on the
colonel's body were documents outlining Dahlgren's in-

tention that Richmond "must be destroyed and Jeff Davis and his cabinet killed." (Most historians now dismiss the papers as forgeries.)

Such military aims seemed "uncivilized" to Virginians. A wave of indignation spread across the state. The Kilpatrick raid had the reverse effect of bolstering Confederate morale. Nevertheless, higher spirits could not withstand the unprecedented Federal hammering that came with springtime.

The Confederate government by then regarded Lee as a miracle man. He was expected to produce victories with dwindling manpower and supplies. Since mobility was imperative for the smaller Confederate army, Lee could not stand toe-to-toe with the Army of the Potomac and slug it out for any length of time.

Lee's strategy, born of resolve, was to "risk some points in order to have a sufficient force concentrated, with the hope of dealing a successful blow when opportunity favors." He was further convinced that "as the enemy cannot attack all points at one time . . . the troops could be concentrated . . . where an assault should be made."

In the spring of 1864 the aging idol of the South found himself taking on a sixth opponent who was the hero of the hour in the North. General Ulysses S. Grant had assumed command of all Union forces. He was of a decidedly different mold from the cautious McClellan and the boastful Hooker. The Civil War had passed the early stage where it might have ended with a negotiated peace. Now it was a fight to the end, with no quarter asked or given. As one of the first tacticians of what is called modern war, Grant introduced in Virginia a type of brutal offensive which eventually would bring this long contest to an end.

A Federal staff officer once commented that in spite of a small stature and plain dress, Grant always had "an expression as if he had determined to drive his head through a brick wall, and was about to do it." His strategy in 1864 reflected such resoluteness. Grant had the idea—radical for that day—that if pressure was applied to all points of the Confederacy, the weak nation could not hold at every point. A fatal rupture would occur somewhere. Late in April he issued orders for Union armies to advance on the South from several directions.

Grant announced that he would join the Army of the Potomac and personally oversee the offensive in Virginia. The new campaign would not be a case of simply fighting a major battle in hopes of victory. Rather, four separate Federal hosts would strike Virginia. The destruction of Lee's army, not the capture of Richmond, was the major objective. Union forces would continue exerting pressure for as long as it took to bring Virginia—and the Confederacy—to their knees.

Grant's war plan was to prevent precisely the kind of concentration that Lee sought. The 1864 war in the Old Dominion became a contest between a boxing lightweight and a slugging heavyweight. But for the genius of Lee and the devotion to duty of his pitiful forces, it would have been no contest at all.

Federal might unloaded on Virginia early in May. Two divisions of infantry and cavalry under Gen. Franz Sigel moved into the Shenandoah Valley to secure that agriculturally rich sector. General Benjamin F. Butler and his 30,000-man army left Fort Monroe and started up the James River in a small but powerful flotilla. Butler's orders were to cut the railroad between Richmond and Petersburg and threaten one or both cities. Grant, accompanying the 115,000 men in the Army of the Potomac, advanced to the south side of the Rapidan to do battle with Lee. The Confederates opposing him numbered 64,000 ragged soldiers. Lee did not contest Grant's crossing of the river. He preferred to attack the Federals in the seventy-two-square-mile wooded entanglement of the Wilderness. There numerical superiority would be nullified, artillery would be useless, and strategy would boil down to who struck first and hardest. Grant's army was strung out for miles along the major country road leading south when, on May 5, Lee sent the corps of Ewell and A. P. Hill assaulting from the west along parallel roads.

For two days vicious fighting raged for control of the intersections of three dirt roads inside the dark forest. Maneuvering by troops in the dense woods was impossible. Regiments fell apart into small groups; oftentimes pairs of soldiers struggled in combat. Officers could only guess the location of battle lines by the roar of gunfire. Back and forth the two armies lunged as smoke and blood and the screams of wounded men covered the Wilderness. Heavy musketry set patches of dry woods and underbrush afire, with the result that scores of injured soldiers too weak to move were cremated.

Longstreet's corps reinforced the hard-pressed Confederate army at a critical moment. Lee was so excited by this timely arrival that he attempted personally to lead the head of those troops in a counterattack. That van, composed in the main of a Texas brigade, immediately shouted: "Lee to the rear! Lee to the rear!" Only after Lee backed off did the Texans charge. They took heavy losses but stabilized the Confederate line.

By nightfall of May 6 Grant's forces had sustained 18,000 casualties. The Army of the Potomac once again had taken a beating. In the past, this had always meant

Fires raged out of control during the battle of the Wilderness.
Century War Book

retreat; but not this time. Grant knew that Lee too had suffered heavy losses (in excess of 10,000 men). The Union ranks could be replenished; Lee's army could not. "Whatever happens," Grant informed Lincoln, "there will be no turning back." So the unflappable Federal general chomped on his cigar, shook off the pain of the Wilderness, and began "sidling" to the southeast to get between Lee and Richmond.

Both armies dashed for Spotsylvania. It was only a sleepy village a dozen miles from the Wilderness; but a number of roads converged there, and to lose it would seriously endanger Lee's lines of communication. The Confederates barely won the race. As the opposing forces came back together, both armies began throwing up earthworks in the usual manner.

For almost two weeks, May 8–21, artillery fire and infantry attacks occurred around Spotsylvania. The worst of the fighting came near the midway point. It was a day of fog, rain, and heavy skies that together could not blanket a killing time terrifying by the standards of any war.

Lee's five miles of defensive works constituted some of the strongest field fortifications of the war. Yet there was a weak sector near the center. Works protruded in a U-shaped "mule shoe" in advance of the main line. This salient was about a mile deep and a half-mile wide. It was a tempting target.

Beginning at dawn on May 12, lines of Federals charged through rain and mud. Savage combat roared unchecked for some twenty hours in what became the longest sustained action of the Civil War. The scene was one of fighting madness. Disciplined soldiers became like wild men. Muskets with bayonets but no bullets were hurled like spears. The living trampled on the wounded and dying. Confederates and Federals slugged it out at such close range that along a 500-yard portion of Lee's line, only the mound of earth in front of the trenches separated friend from foe. A twenty-two-inch oak tree fell to the ground from rifle fire alone.

Afterwards a Johnny Reb sent a hasty note to his wife: "The battle of thursday was one of the bloodiest that ever dyed God's foot-table with human gore." Each side lost about 7,000 men that day at the "Bloody Angle." Confederates later gathered up 120,000 pounds of lead from the battlefield. Lee had managed to keep his lines intact but at a frightful cost. In addition to the dead and wounded, huge chunks of Jackson's old corps had been captured. The invalid Mrs. Robert E. Lee stated in anguish at her Richmond home: "What will my poor husband do? It seems God has turned His face from us."

Her husband found little comfort from his victories in the first half of May. Southern knighthood was no match for Northern manpower. Every battle, regardless of its outcome, sapped strength from the Army of Northern Virginia. The Wilderness-Spotsylvania fighting was especially crippling for Lee. Of his three corps commanders, Longstreet was down with wounds and both Ewell and Hill were sick. Lee's own health was deteriorating from the cares of war. For Lee the general, the worst aspect of the campaign was that he was too locked in combat now to do the maneuvering at which he was so skillful—and Grant showed no disposition to let go.

Grant, on the other hand, had reason to pause at Spotsylvania. Federal losses in Virginia had been greater in the past two weeks than anywhere else in any other comparable period of the struggle. Not only had Grant suffered the two bloodiest setbacks of his career; two of the three simultaneous Federal drives in other parts of Virginia had failed.

The one sign of encouragement for Grant during the Spotsylvania campaign was a mounted raid on Richmond. Union cavalry had been consolidated under di-

The May 12, 1864, fighting at Spotsylvania's "Bloody Angle." *Century War Book*

munitive but hard-boiled Gen. Philip H. Sheridan. On May 8 Grant ordered the second strike at the capital within two months. Sheridan's instructions were to disrupt Lee's communications with Richmond and pull Stuart's horsemen away from the Confederate army.

Some 13,000 Federal cavalry cut a swath of destruc-

General Philip H. Sheridan (1831–1888), as he looked in the postwar years. *The Soldier in Our Civil War*

tion as they leisurely rode southward toward the capital. Sheridan hoped that Stuart's 4,000 ill-equipped horsemen would accept the challenge for battle. Stuart gave chase; and on May 11 at Yellow Tavern on Richmond's northern outskirts the two bands crashed together. Sheridan's superior numbers and firepower overwhelmed the Confederate cavalry. In the midst of the action, an unhorsed Michigan cavalryman saw a big enemy officer with his red-lined cape and flowing beard. The Yankee fired his revolver.

Jeb Stuart reeled in the saddle long enough to shout to his men: "Go back and do your duty as I have done mine and the country will be saved!" His men took the mortally wounded general home to Richmond to die. Jackson had perished the previous May. Now it was

Stuart. The gaiety and youthfulness of the Confederacy seemed to die with the cavalry chief about whom Lee could only say: "He never brought me a piece of false information."

Sheridan's victory at Yellow Tavern ended the raid. Aware that he could not take Richmond with his limited numbers, Sheridan led his troopers through a driving rain and took shelter with Butler's army south of the James River.

The other two Federal thrusts in Virginia were embarrassing failures. General Franz Sigel's movements in the Shenandoah ended at New Market. On May 15, a makeshift force of 5,000 Confederates attacked Sigel's 6,500 Federals. In the middle of the assault were 247 teenaged cadets from the Virginia Military Institute. These "little devils," as Sigel called them, helped overrun the Union position and send the Federal expedition in full retreat. The VMI cadets returned to Lexington with the only battle flag ever captured by a college student body.

At precisely the same time, Benjamin Butler and his Federal Army of the James were in the process of coming up even more empty-handed. Butler's failure was particularly galling because he blundered enough to snatch defeat from the jaws of victory. Three targets lay in front of Butler's unobstructed advance. Richmond was the primary goal. Twenty-two miles south of the capital was the smaller town of Petersburg, a rail junction which connected Richmond with what was left of the Confederacy. Squarely between the two cities was Drewry's Bluff, the only James River fort protecting Richmond from Union gunboats. No organized Southern units were in the area. The bits and pieces available for defense were inadequate.

Opposing cavalry fight at Yellow Tavern. *Harper's Weekly*

Butler made a truly sorry performance. He took his troops by boat up the James to within fifteen miles of Richmond. They disembarked, marched a few miles, and made weak stabs at the Richmond-Petersburg rail line. The Union general could have taken Petersburg with ease; Richmond might have fallen with minimum effort on the part of the Federals. Butler sat down for awhile between the two, trying to make up his mind. He lost both objectives by deciding to attack Drewry's Bluff.

Getting into position proved a laborious task. On May 16, as Butler was completing his battle preparations, he was assaulted by a large conglomerate of Confederates under Gen. P. G. T. Beauregard of Fort Sumter and First Manassas fame. Butler fell back in the rain and took cover inside a peninsula at the confluence of the James and Appomattox rivers. The opening across that neck of land was only four miles wide. Beauregard skillfully constructed a seal of fortifications across the entrance and packed his forces in battle position. A disgusted Grant stated that Butler's army was "completely shut off from further operations" directly against Richmond because it had put itself "in a bottle strongly corked."

The Union general-in-chief was now alone in his offensive against Lee's forces. Grant abandoned the Spotsylvania line and attempted another flank march around the Confederate right. As he did so, Lee shifted his forces on shorter interior lines and confronted Grant anew at the North Anna River. Federal probes at the river crossings met enough resistance to discourage thoughts of any full-scale attack. Grant might have come to a different decision if he had known that his opponent was ailing. Lee by then was so ill from a combination of heart disease and diarrhea that he could not ride a horse. He was directing army operations from a carriage.

In the last week of May, Grant moved still again to the southeast. Federals made a twenty-mile swing across the Pamunkey River and approached the area where the Seven Days' battles of two years earlier had begun. Lee countermarched, again using the inside track. The Confederates were now dangerously close to the northeastern limits of Richmond. Another, briefer race occurred for a strategic road intersection known as Cold Harbor. Lee got there first, attacked on June 1, but failed to gain any ground.

With Federal plans once more foiled, and with Lee's troops seemingly stretched out in an overly long line, Grant impatiently and erroneously concluded that he had a good chance to smash the Southern army. He ordered a frontal attack at Cold Harbor with confidence that it would succeed. Veteran soldiers chosen to make the assault knew better. Before the battle, hundreds of Billy Yanks wrote their names and addresses on slips of paper and pinned them to their shirts so that burial details would be able to identify their bodies. Found on one dead Federal afterwards was a simple note: "June 3. Cold Harbor. I was killed."

Lee's 50,000 men had, in truth, taken maximum advantage of every ravine, stream, and tree line. Rarely in war has a defender laid down such a concentrated fire as Lee was able to do at Cold Harbor. Over 7,000 Federals were killed or wounded, most of them in the first hour of fighting. A colonel who fell dead across a parapet was hit by so many stray bullets that when his body was recovered a few days later, he could be identified only by the buttons on his sleeve.

A loud outcry of horror and rage echoed through the

North. Grant's generalship in one month had cost the Union 60,000 casualties, which was almost as many men as Lee had at the outset of the campaign in May. Grant was no closer to Richmond than McClellan had been two years ago. Even worse for Northern morale, the apparently indifferent general from Illinois who had stated at Spotsylvania, "I propose to fight it out on this line if it takes all summer," still maintained that resolve.

While the dead at Cold Harbor went unburied, and the wounded still cried for help, Grant studied his options. His hope from the beginning had been to bring Lee to battle in open country. Lee was too limited in manpower by 1864 to accept such a contest. The Confederate army seemed disposed to fight henceforth from trenches.

Grant concluded to unite with Butler's army and seize Petersburg, the vital underbelly of Richmond. That would not bring about the immediate fall of either the capital or Lee's army, but it would isolate Richmond and begin its death vigil. Moreover, the country around Petersburg was flat and open—good fighting ground and void of those wide streams that had so far hampered Grant all the way through Virginia.

In mid-June, Grant disappeared from Lee's front in a final flanking movement. The Union army crossed the James on the longest pontoon bridge ever constructed (2,200 yards). A fresh Federal corps went forward to take Petersburg. Inside the city were Beauregard's 2,500 irregulars. Yet they were behind formidable works that disguised their weak numbers. The Federal attacks were hesitant and uncoordinated. After three days of weak jabs, Beauregard's men still clung precariously to their defenses. It was Beauregard's finest hour as a Confeder-

General Lee in 1863, aged by dwindling Confederate forces, heavy Federal pressure, and frequent personal illnesses. The Museum of the Confederacy, courtesy of the Virginia Historical Society, Richmond

ate general. On June 18 the Army of Northern Virginia began filing into the Petersburg works.

Lee and Grant were facing each other again. However, the struggle for Virginia had changed drastically since the two men first locked horns in the Wilderness. While Lee had not lost battles, neither had he won the campaign. Lee had thwarted Grant's designs, but he had been unable to effect any designs of his own. The 32,000 losses suffered by Lee in the past six weeks represented half of his Confederate army. A third of his generals had been killed or wounded in the fighting that spring. The soldiers who remained were staggering from exhaustion and want as they took new positions in the Petersburg line.

Grant also knew something about earthworks. His forces were soon so well entrenched that Lee could not possibly dislodge them. Worst of all for Lee, what was beginning at Petersburg was a major siege—something Grant had used to smashing success at Vicksburg the previous summer. Siege warfare was a static contest which Lee could not win.

From the beginning of the Wilderness campaign, Lee's objective had been to stand between Grant and Richmond but always maneuvering to make maximum use of his inferior forces. Mobility had been his great strategic advantage. Now Lee could scarcely move. When he could, his numbers were too insufficient to be a serious threat. Immediately behind Lee was Richmond, the fortress he was duty-bound to defend to the last. The defiant capital, for three years the magnet for Federal armies, had become a millstone for Lee to bear. He was immobilized and held by a short chain.

The Confederate army that had for so long swung through woods, across rivers, over mountains, and slashed here and there at the enemy, had struck through three states in unforgettable campaigns, now was pinned down in the heat, filth, want, and stench of the Petersburg trenches. The months ahead would see the once-proud and formidable Army of Northern Virginia reduced to what its own members called "Lee's Miserables."

. XI .

End of a Dream

While Grant was marching toward Cold Harbor, he ordered a second and larger effort made to isolate the Shenandoah Valley from the rest of Virginia. General David Hunter entered the region with 22,000 Federals. The narrow-eyed, scowling Hunter had roots in the Valley; he also had a hatred of the slave South which overrode his respect for heritage. Billy Yanks followed his lead and wrecked everything in their path.

They saved their greatest vengeance for Lexington. Every building but one at VMI was put to the torch. The Washington College library was burned, along with the homes of Gov. John Letcher and other prominent citizens. A Union soldier commented at the time: "Many women look sad and do much weeping over the destruction that is going on. We feel that the South brought on the war and the State of Virginia is paying dear for her part."

Hunter turned east toward Lynchburg, a central Virginia town of some importance with two railroads and several military hospitals. Both Lee and Grant then made chess moves to strengthen contending forces in the piedmont. Lee dispatched two brigades from his army under feisty Gen. Jubal Early to reinforce the Lynchburg defenders. Grant ordered Sheridan's cavalry to ride toward Hunter and tear up the Virginia Central Railroad en route. Lee did not want Sheridan and Hunter to unite, for such a force could move on Richmond or on

Lee's rear. A Confederate cavalry detachment under Gen. Wade Hampton galloped off in hot pursuit of Sheridan.

On June 11–12 no more than 5,000 Southern horsemen engaged 9,000 Federal cavalry at Trevilian Station in one of the bloodiest mounted fights of the war. The battle was a draw; but with Hunter still ninety miles to the west, Sheridan abandoned his movement and returned to Grant.

Hunter was now unsupported, low on ammunition, and running out of enthusiasm. His army arrived on the western edge of Lynchburg to find a sizable force of angry Confederates. Hunter tried to retire in order; however, with the Valley retreat blocked by guerrilla bands and "Old Jube" Early biting at his heels, Hunter's withdrawal became a near-rout. Federals scurried to safety in the mountains of West Virginia.

The aggressive Early was not finished. In the first week of July, Early embarked on a daring offensive of his own with the hope of diverting some of Grant's forces. His 13,000 mostly barefooted men marched down the Valley and crossed the Potomac. They brushed aside a small force at Monocacy, Md., on July 9 and two days later were in battle line on the northwestern outskirts of Washington.

Early's band was too small to do more than send fear through the streets of the Northern capital for a couple of days. In that respect, the raid was successful. Early returned to the Shenandoah with satisfaction at the blow he had delivered to self-respect and feelings of security in the North.

An exasperated Grant now took action. From Petersburg he organized a third—and this time major—drive to neutralize once and for all the "Breadbasket of the

Confederacy." His most dependable lieutenant, "Little Phil" Sheridan, with 40,000 seasoned veterans left for Winchester and Early's entrenched army. Grant's instructions to Sheridan were explicit: "Do all the damage to railroads and crops you can. . . . If the war is to last another year, we want the Shenandoah Valley to remain a barren waste."

On September 19 Sheridan met Early at Opequon Creek. The Federal attack got off to a shaky start when

General David Hunter (1802–1886). Library of Congress

General Jubal A. Early (1816–
1894). *Century War Book*

an infantry corps became hopelessly ensnared in its own
wagon train. Yet Sheridan pressed forward with superior numbers and carried the field. Three days later, Federals drove through Early's new position at Fisher's Hill,
killed or captured a third of the Confederate force, and
sent the remainder in full retreat. Sheridan was now free
to begin a systematic devastation of the Shenandoah. He
stated in a communiqué to Grant that when he finished
his work, "the Valley, from Winchester up to Staunton,
ninety-two miles, will have little in it for man or beast."

The Federal general proved as tough as his words.
Over 2,000 barns and 70 mills were burned. When Sheridan received a false report that guerrillas had killed one
of his officers, he ordered all homes within a five-mile
area set afire. Federals seized or destroyed 435,800

bushels of wheat, 3,800 horses, 10,900 cattle, 12,000 sheep, 77,000 bushels of corn, 12,000 pounds of bacon, 20,400 tons of hay, plus all else that had any value to the rapidly weakening resistance in Virginia. That autumn a War Department clerk in Richmond noted in his diary: "Through the efforts of Sheridan's raid, Richmond is rapidly approaching a state of famine."

Lee rushed 3,600 troops from Petersburg as a transfusion to Early's skeletal army. In desperation, Early made an early-morning surprise attack on October 19 at Cedar Creek against part of the Union forces. The Confederates were outnumbered two to one, but the suddenness of the assault sent some 7,000 Federals fleeing in panic. Early ordered his troops to push forward to complete victory. However, large numbers of hungry Rebels stopped to plunder the abandoned Federal camps.

Early's drive began to lose momentum just as Sheridan galloped onto the field and began rallying his fugitives. A furious counterattack caught the Southerners in about as disorganized a condition as a major Confederate force had ever been. Large groups surrendered on the field; others scampered southward in headlong flight. Cedar Creek was the last major event in the Valley. The region was permanently under Federal control. Its great yield of foodstuffs was no longer available to Lee.

Throughout the summer and autumn, meantime, Grant had doggedly tightened his grip on Lee's army. His operations at Petersburg began in earnest with one of the more unusual assaults of the war. Coal miners in a Pennsylvania regiment dug a 511-foot tunnel underneath "no-man's land" to a salient in Lee's center. They filled the end with 8,000 pounds of gunpowder. The en-

The "Battle of the Crater," depicting Confederates counterattacking and driving Federals from the gigantic hole created by the underground explosion. *Century War Book*

suing explosion on July 30 blew a gaping hole in the Confederate works. About 15,000 Federals (including black soldiers seeing their first combat action in Virginia) attacked amid the smoke and confusion of the blast. Confederates beat back the assaults at a cost of 1,500 men. This "Battle of the Crater" cost 4,000 Union losses and convinced Grant of the futility of frontal assaults against Lee's defenses at Petersburg.

Lee and Grant realized that the siege at Petersburg was not merely a showdown between them, or between their armies. This was going to be a death struggle between the Union and the Confederacy. By that stage of the war, such a contest lopsidedly favored the stronger side.

Sam Grant's strategy at Petersburg was a simple and deadly effective three-step process. First, Grant knew that time was on his side. He accordingly increased his ranks and stockpiled the Federal army for a long siege. The Union supply base was on the James River at City Point (now Hopewell), a harbor to which the U.S. Navy could proceed unmolested. Engineers constructed a twenty-one-mile rail line from the docks to the very rear of Grant's entrenchments. They did it quicker and with more ease than strapped Confederates could repair a half-mile segment of the railroad between Richmond and Petersburg. Federal strength increased steadily thereafter while Lee's army just as steadily became smaller.

Next, Grant sought to starve Richmond and its defenders by severing the railroads heading west and south from Petersburg. Union cavalry began hacking at the lines until their use was measured by how crippled they were. When Federals in August broke the Petersburg and Weldon Railroad, Lee was reduced to using wagons to haul supplies the last twenty miles to his men.

Lastly, Grant dealt directly with Lee by utilizing ingredients that the Southern commander could not stop: constant pressure and weight of numbers. The Federal general employed a pendulum action against the Southern position. Grant would strike first one end of Lee's line and then the other, all the time pounding away in the center at Petersburg. Lee's units each time had to drop shovels, grab muskets, and rush to meet every threat. All the while, artillery barrages and sharpshooter fire came from all sectors of the Union lines.

These pendulum movements swung back and forth, week after week. Grant's superiority in numbers was usually two or three to one. Lee's watchfulness was such, and his handling of his crippled army so masterly, that while Grant was always free to choose his point of attack, he was never able to accumulate sufficient strength to crash through Lee's defenses. Whenever Grant tried, he lost more men than Lee. Each time Grant brought up replacements; each time Lee had fewer troops. For the Southern army, it was a slow hemorrhaging.

By autumn 1864 the siege lines stretched from White Oak Swamp east of Richmond, south to Drewry's Bluff, and across the James in a slow southwestern arc to the far side of Petersburg. Large-scale actions occurred at Fort Harrison on Lee's left and at the Southside Railroad and Boydton Plank Road on Lee's right. The land borders of the Confederacy had once extended from the Atlantic Ocean to the Mexican border. As the year came to a close, the only stable battlefront in the South was the Richmond-Petersburg line of barely thirty miles.

Winter came early and hard. The Army of Northern Virginia had never known the misery that followed.

Dirty, cold men lived in crude lean-tos and mud caves behind the trenches. Firewood was scarce. Johnny Rebs in the front lines had 18 rounds per man, while Federal pickets at the same time were complaining because they were required to fire 100 rounds daily at something.

Worse, days passed when no food was available for the Rebels. Underfed horses could no longer pull wagons. Troops survived on whatever they could obtain. Federal general Butler stated after the war: "The fact is incontestable that a soldier in our army would have quite easily starved on the rations . . . served out to the Confederate soldiers before Petersburg."

Desertions increased markedly during the winter months. Brave soldiers who had stood with Lee for the entire war lost heart and at night either crept over to the Federal lines or simply wandered away toward home. Mrs. Phoebe Pember in Richmond could not condemn the brave men who now deserted. "How hard for the husband to remain inactive in winter quarters knowing that his wife and little ones were literally starving at home—not even at home, for few homes were left." Lee's once-fearsome brigades dwindled into a half-starved, half-naked collection of men clinging to their battle flags. The haunting faces that filled Lee's ranks were a painful omen that the end was approaching.

Grant applied Union pressure relentlessly. Hourly picket fire echoed up and down the line. Never was there a day of silence; never was there a day without casualties. Northern manpower was such that Grant continued fighting his way slowly westward to cut off the last road from the south and the remaining open railroad from Petersburg. Lee countered each Federal extension of the line by stretching his own line farther to the west. Doing so forced the Confederate general to increase the danger for the areas from which he had taken men. The siege lines were soon thirty-seven miles long. No more than 35,000 worn-out Southerners faced an army of 124,000 well-equipped troops. Johnny Rebs manning some earthworks stood paces apart. Lee's position resembled a rubber band stretching slowly, inexorably to the breaking point.

It came on March 31, 1865, six days after Lee's feeble attempt to puncture the Union line at Fort Stedman had failed. Grant delivered a long-awaited hammer blow against Lee's extreme right. Somehow the Confederate line held. The next day, heavily reinforced, Federals charged again through the mud at Five Forks and this time shattered Lee's flank.

Grant now unloosed the full might of his army. Federal artillery, from the Appomattox River to Five Forks, spent the night of April 1–2 blasting Lee's position with the heaviest bombardment of the entire war. Flashing guns and shell explosions turned the night into day; the ground trembled all the way to Richmond. With dawn came massive Federal attacks at several points.

The Confederate line broke under the onslaught. General A. P. Hill, Lee's principal lieutenant throughout the siege, fell dead early in the fighting. Although the Southerners managed to make a stand from the inner ring of Petersburg's defenses, this gained only a few hours for the evacuation of Richmond. Jefferson Davis and a handful of Confederate officials took the last train from the capital for Danville.

Mobs soon filled Richmond's streets. Looting and other crimes became rampant. Confederate soldiers dutifully set fire to warehouses and government stores to prevent their capture. Winds arose after midnight, flames jumped from building to building, and by dawn

Grant's massive assaults at the beginning of April 1865, too strong for the thin Confederate line to withstand. *Harper's Weekly*

of April 3 the heart of Richmond's commercial district was on fire. An estimated 900 businesses and homes were destroyed. It was a cruel death for the Confederate capital.

Lee took the remnant of his forces and marched slowly to the west. His objective was to reach the Richmond and Danville Railroad and to follow it to Danville, the temporary capital and a town whose hills offered a good defensive position. Yet Federal cavalry galloped ahead of Lee and got astride the railroad. Lee veered to the northwest in hopes of reaching Lynchburg. His men staggered along unfamiliar roads. Exhausted Johnny Rebs hardly knew day from night. Meanwhile, Grant's pursuit was relentless. Blue-clad horsemen harassed Lee's flanks, while Union infantry snapped every mile at Lee's rear.

The most famous depiction of Lee's surrender to Grant at Appomattox. *Century War Book*

In a sharp fight at Sayler's Creek on April 6, Federals overwhelmed a third of the Confederate army. About 8,000 men were lost to add to the hundreds dropping daily from the ranks because of hunger, fatigue, and sickness. Lee got his small band as far as Appomattox Court House. There he found his way blocked by lines of Federals. Nothing was left but surrender.

April 9 was Palm Sunday. The two commanders met in the home of Wilmer McLean (who had moved to Appomattox from Manassas in 1861 to get away from the war). Grant's terms of surrender were more generous than Lee expected, and he accepted them thankfully. The contrast between the two generals that afternoon was pertinent. Lee, in full uniform with sword and sash, represented the pride and martial spirit that had been the Old South. Grant, in a plain, mud-spattered uniform almost void of any show of rank, reflected the unfettered strength of an industrial North.

To Confederate soldiers weeping openly, Lee made a final written announcement. It stated in part: "With an unceasing admiration of your constancy and devotion to your Country, and grateful remembrance of your kind and generous consideration of myself, I bid you all an affectionate farewell. . . . You will take with you the satisfaction that proceeds from the consciousness of duty faithfully performed; and I earnestly pray that a Merciful God will extend to you His blessings and protection."

Appomattox made the phrase "United States" a fact. The nation still had a long way to go before unity became the equal of liberty. Yet no other civil war has ended so peacefully. No nation has been given a more honorable second chance.

Robert E. Lee departed from Appomattox as the first

Lee saying goodbye to his troops after surrendering his army.
Century War Book

American general to lose a war; but as he rode away from defeat, Lee carried the Army of Northern Virginia, the image of the "Lost Cause," and the Southern people with him straight into legend.

. XII .

A *Living Heritage*

The North fought the contest removed from the scene of action and with little danger to its interior. The South, on the other hand, caught the full fury of the Civil War. Virginia suffered worst of all. It had been the site of more than 200 military engagements. Over a half-million men had been killed, wounded, or captured in the Old Dominion during the four years of combat.

From one end of the state to the other, the situation in the spring of 1865 was the same: houses and businesses destroyed, fields ruined, crops and livestock confiscated, streams contaminated, bridges wrecked. Countless homes were charred skeletons of past splendor. Lee's homestead at Arlington, confiscated by Federals at Viriginia's secession, was on its way to becoming the nation's most famous national cemetery.

Most of Virginia's urban areas lay in shambles. All of Fredericksburg and the heart of Richmond were in ashes; Petersburg lay pockmarked from nine months of bombardment; Norfolk was a wasteland whose streets resembled avenues of potholes; Bristol, Wytheville, and Winchester were badly scarred from attacks; Warrenton, Culpeper, Lynchburg, Danville, and a dozen other towns had a general air of neglect and filth.

A Northerner traveling through Virginia shortly after Lee's surrender beheld "no sign of human industry, save here and there a sickly, half-cultivated corn field." He added that "the country for the most part consisted of

fenceless fields abandoned to weeds, stump lots and undergrowth." That same spring a Culpeper farmer, whose
land had been ravaged by contending armies moving
back and forth over it, stated: "I hain't took no sides in
this yer rebellion, but I'll be dog-garned if both sides
hain't took me."

Greater than the material destruction to the state was
the loss of life. Some 20,000 to 30,000 Virginia soldiers
were dead. Thousands of others hobbled along city
streets and country roads with an arm or leg missing.
Even larger numbers of veterans never recovered from
the effects of wartime diseases and hardships. An ines-
timable number of soldiers who had deserted the army
mainly because of deprivations at home had to live with
their shame. How many innocent citizens had been
killed in the cross fire of skirmishes and battles is incal-
culable. In short, two generations of Virginians were
maimed beyond description.

Virginia's economic system was shattered. Confederate bonds and currency were worthless; reliable cash
was nonexistent. So widespread was the devastation
that six months after the war ended, 25,000 Virginia
citizens were still receiving daily army rations as a
means of survival. At the same time, most of the
360,000 now-freed blacks wandered aimlessly along
city streets and rural backroads.

The future held no promise. An age of great plantations was history. By the end of the 1860s land selling
for $50 per acre before the war could be bought for $2
per acre. Estates of 1,000 acres or more were only half
the number that had been flourishing in 1860. The
state's industrial production was so shattered that Virginia was the only Southern state that failed by 1870 to
reach prewar levels. War, military occupation, and fed-

The blackened, burned-out blocks of downtown Richmond in
April 1865. Eleanor S. Brockenbrough Library, The Museum of the
Confederacy

erally-imposed "reconstruction" reduced Virginia to
near-vassalage. The "Mother of States" endured and ultimately prospered through a combination of pride in
yesterday and determination for tomorrow.

In 1880 Virginia-born and future president Woodrow
Wilson made an observation: "*Because* I love the South,
I rejoice in the failure of the Confederacy. . . . Conceive
of this Union divided into two separate and independent
sovereignties! . . . [Nevertheless] I recognize and pay
tribute to the virtues of the leaders of secession . . . the
righteousness of the cause which they thought they were
promoting—and to the immortal courage of the soldiers
of the Confederacy."

No soldier of the South stands taller in remembrance than Robert E. Lee. Selfless to a fault, and despite failing health, the defeated general accepted the presidency of impoverished Washington College at Lexington. Lee spent his remaining energies in training young men—as well as their parents—to forget animosities and to become good Americans. "General Lee's College" became a model for higher education in the postwar South. It is now called Washington and Lee University. At the general's death in 1870, the entire nation paid tribute. Julia Ward Howe, whose pen had given the Union the stirring lines of "The Battle Hymn of the Republic," wrote movingly of Lee:

The recumbent statue of Lee, by Edward V. Valentine, above Lee's
burial vault. Washington and Lee University

A gallant foeman in the fight,
A brother when the fight was o'er . . .
And so, thy soldier grave beside,
We honor thee, Virginia's son.

Virginia's contributions to the Confederate high command were dominant. Lee and Joseph Johnston were
among the eight full generals. Jackson, A. P. Hill, and

Early gained the rank of lieutenant general. Twenty-three Virginians became major generals, while seventy-one others attained brigadier general status. One of every five Virginia general officers was killed or mortally wounded in action.

The Confederate States Navy similarly had a large representation of Virginians. Matthew Fontaine Maury was the state's most famous maritime figure. John Randolph Tucker was an outstanding commander of both the CSS *Patrick Henry* and the CSS *Chicora*. A host of other officers made indelible marks on naval history: captains Archibald B. Fairfax, French Forrest, Catesby ap R. Jones, Sidney Smith Lee, William F. Lynch, Robert B. Pegram, Arthur Sinclair, William C. Whittle, plus

Matthew Fontaine Maury (1806–1873), photographed by Matthew Brady. The Museum of the Confederacy, courtesy of the Library of Congress

lieutenants John Mercer Brooke, William L. Maury, and James H. Rochelle.

Fittingly in that war, seventeen Virginians (including Winfield Scott, George H. Thomas, and Philip St. George Cooke) became Union generals. Commodore William Radford, six captains, and eleven commanders—all from Virginia—played prominent roles in the U.S. Navy.

More than half of the state's male population served in some military capacity. Virginia Confederate units included one regiment, eight battalions, and ninety-six companies of artillery, twenty-five regiments and twenty-two battalions of cavalry, sixty-two regiments and thirteen battalions of infantry, three regiments, seven battalions, and scores of companies organized under Local Defense Troops, plus State Rangers, the Virginia State Line, Home Guard, and Reserves.

A number of state organizations achieved a fame saluted by troops on both sides. Hill's Light Division, the Stonewall Brigade, the Old First Regiment, Richmond Howitzers, Pegram's Artillery Battalion, and Mosby's Rangers were but a few. Some units gained memorable records through extraordinary losses in a single engagement. At the battle of Antietam Creek, the 15th Virginia Infantry lost 58.8 percent of its command, the 17th suffered 56.3 percent casualties, and the 32nd incurred 45.5 percent losses. The 4th Virginia of the Stonewall Brigade took 53.8 percent losses at First Manassas and 48.8 percent in killed and wounded at Chancellorsville. General Richard B. Garnett's Virginia troops led all Confederate brigades in highest casualties in a single battle: 65.9 percent in the Pickett-Pettigrew charge at Gettysburg. Garnett himself was killed in the famous assault.

A tattered Confederate battle flag, emblazoned with the word "Chancellorsville," bearing mute testimony to the severity of the war in Virginia. The Museum of the Confederacy

The road to recovery over the past 125 years has been long, difficult, but ultimately successful. Reconstruction and its failures had several effects. The abortive Confederacy came in time to rise from disastrous defeat to the honorable status of a "Lost Cause." Starting from the ashes of war, Virginia spent a century trying to catch up with development in the North and West. Legislated segregation crippled race relations for decades.

Virginia has shifted dramatically in this century from a rural and agricultural region to a predominantly urban and industrialized society. Office buildings and factories in great part have replaced farmlands; suburbia is the way of life for a majority of Virginia citizens. The "New

Dominion," as many call the state, is vibrant and prosperous. The most sterling symbol of reconciliation may have been the 1989 election of L. Douglas Wilder, a grandson of slaves and the first black ever elected governor of a state.

Today Virginia thinks of the present and plans for the future; but more so than most states, Virginia cherishes the past. To begin to forget, Virginians had first to remember and to pay tribute. The state has done that in a number of visible ways.

A dozen of the major battlefields are at least partly preserved, thanks to untiring efforts by the National Park Service and—in several instances—the Commonwealth of Virginia. Other important battle arenas still exist as they were, but many of them stand in peril because of the greed of developers. Ground sanctified by the blood and tears of patriots deserves a better fate.

Statues in bronze and granite watch from courthouse lawns, boulevards, graveyards, and town squares. Stone memorials, roadside markers, historical societies, and museums can be found in almost every county. Spread across the state too are a number of soldier-cemeteries. There men who loved their country more than they loved their lives now rest in the last sleep. The silence of those fields bespeaks a legacy that is the United States of America.

Modern-day citizens and visitors in Virginia can learn much and profit more from the lessons of the Civil War. Seeking a better understanding of that struggle would be the greatest tribute we could pay to the men of blue and gray, as well as to the nation they forged, not for themselves alone, but for all Americans now and yet to come.

Selected Bibliography

Allan, William. *The Army of Northern Virginia in 1862*. Reprint: Dayton, Ohio: Morningside Bookshop, 1984.

———. *History of the Campaign of Gen. T. J. (Stonewall) Jackson in the Shenandoah Valley of Virginia*. Reprint: Dayton, Ohio: Morningside House, 1987.

Boney, F. N. *John Letcher of Virginia*. University: University of Alabama Press, 1966.

Catton, Bruce. *Glory Road*. Garden City, N.Y.: Doubleday, 1952.

———. *Mr. Lincoln's Army*. Garden City, N.Y.: Doubleday, 1951.

———. *A Stillness at Appomattox*. Garden City, N.Y.: Doubleday, 1953.

Chambers, Lenoir. *Stonewall Jackson*. 2 vols. New York: William Morrow, 1959.

Cole, Garold L. *Civil War Eyewitnesses: An Annotated Bibliography of Books and Articles, 1955–1986*. Columbia: University of South Carolina Press, 1988.

Cunningham, H. H. *Doctors in Gray*. Baton Rouge: Louisiana State University Press, 1958.

Dabney, Virginius. *Richmond: The Story of a City*. Garden City, N.Y.: Doubleday, 1976.

———. *Virginia: The New Dominion*. Garden City, N.Y.: Doubleday, 1971.

Davis, William C. *Duel between the First Ironclads*. Garden City, N.Y.: Doubleday, 1975.

Escott, Paul D. *After Secession: Jefferson Davis and the Failure of Confederate Nationalism*. Baton Rouge: Louisiana State University Press, 1978.

Frassanito, William A. *Grant and Lee: The Virginia Campaigns, 1864–1865*. New York: Charles Scribner's Sons, 1983.

Freeman, Douglas Southall. *Lee's Lieutenants: A Study in Command*. 3 vols. New York: Charles Scribner's Sons, 1942–44.

———. *R. E. Lee: A Biography*. 4 vols. New York: Charles Scribner's Sons, 1934–35.

Hesseltine, William B. *Civil War Prisons: A Study in War Psychology*. Columbus: Ohio State University Press, 1930.

Hotchkiss, Jedediah. *Confederate Military History*. Vol. 3. *Virginia*.

Reprints: Dayton, Ohio: Morningside Bookshop, 1975; Wilmington, N.C.: Broadfoot Publishing Company, 1988.

Johnson, Ludwell H. *Division and Reunion: America, 1848–1877.* New York: John Wiley & Sons, 1978.

Johnston, Angus J., II. *Virginia Railroads in the Civil War.* Chapel Hill: University of North Carolina Press, 1961.

Jones, John B. *A Rebel War Clerk's Diary at the Confederate States Capital.* 2 vols. Reprint: Alexandria, Va.: Time-Life Books, 1982.

Jones, Katharine M. *Ladies of Richmond.* Indianapolis: Bobbs-Merrill, 1962.

Long, E. B. *The Civil War Day by Day.* Garden City, N.Y.: Doubleday, 1971.

McDonald, Cornelia P. *A Diary with Reminiscences of the War and Refugee Life in the Shenandoah Valley, 1860–1865.* Nashville: Cullom & Ghertner, 1934.

McPherson, James B. *Battle Cry of Freedom: The Civil War Era.* New York: Oxford University Press, 1988.

Massey, Mary Elizabeth. *Ersatz in the Confederacy.* Columbia: University of South Carolina Press, 1952.

Nevins, Allan, et al., eds. *Civil War Books: A Critical Bibliography.* 2 vols. Reprint: Wilmington, N.C.: Broadfoot Publishing Company, 1988.

Putnam, Sallie B. *Richmond during the War: Four Years of Personal Observation.* Reprint: Alexandria, Va.: Time-Life Books, 1983.

Robertson, James I., Jr. *Civil War Sites in Virginia: A Tour Guide.* Charlottesville: University Press of Virginia, 1982.

——. *Soldiers Blue and Gray.* Columbia: University of South Carolina Press, 1988.

Roland, Charles P. *The Confederacy.* Chicago: University of Chicago Press, 1960.

Thomas, Emory M. *The Confederate State of Richmond.* Austin: University of Texas Press, 1971.

Virginia Civil War Battles and Leaders Series. Lynchburg, Va.: H. E. Howard, 1985– .

Virginia Regimental Histories Series. Lynchburg, Va.: H. E. Howard, 1982– .

Wallace, Lee A., Jr. *A Guide to Virginia Military Organizations, 1861–1865.* Reprint: Lynchburg, Va.: H. E. Howard, 1986.

INDEX

Note: All locales are in Virginia unless otherwise stated.